TIDY UP
YOUR LIFE

TIDY UP YOUR LIFE

Rethinking How to Organize,
Declutter, and Make Space
for What Matters Most

Tyler Moore

RODALE
NEW YORK

Published in the United States by Rodale Books, an imprint of Random House, a division of Penguin Random House LLC, New York.

Rodale & Plant with colophon is a registered trademark of Penguin Random House LLC.

Values Wheel on page 65 is sourced and created by ACT Leadership Corporation (www.actleader.com). Used with permission.

Library of Congress Cataloging-in-Publication Data
Names: Moore, Tyler, author.
Title: Tidy up your life / Tyler Moore.
Description: New York, NY: Rodale, [2025] |
Identifiers: LCCN 2024019982 (print) | LCCN 2024019983 (ebook) |
ISBN 9780593797839 (hardcover) | ISBN 9780593797846 (ebook)
Subjects: LCSH: Storage in the home. | House cleaning. | Mind and body. |
Self-management (Psychology)
Classification: LCC TX324.5 .M66 2025 (print) | LCC TX324.5 (ebook) |
DDC 648/.5—dc23/eng/20240723
LC record available at https://lccn.loc.gov/2024019982
LC ebook record available at https://lccn.loc.gov/2024019983

Printed in the United States of America on acid-free paper

RodaleBooks.com | RandomHouseBooks.com

2 4 6 8 9 7 5 3 1

FIRST EDITION

Book design by Ralph Fowler

To my wife, Emily, and our daughters,
Mabel, Matilda, and Margaret

CONTENTS

PART ONE

TIDY UP YOUR MIND

PART TWO

TIDY UP YOUR SPACE

What I Learned from the Great Bedroom Flip

Over eggs, sausage, and coffee that morning, and amid the squeals of two young children, I'd announced my ingenious plan to my wife, Emily. We were going to switch bedrooms with our kids. We lived in a 750-square-foot apartment in Queens, and after welcoming Matilda home to her older sister, Mabel, we'd questioned how we were going to make the small apartment work with four of us. We loved where we lived. After all, New York City is the "concrete jungle where dreams are made of." But things felt cramped. So, my thinking was that Emily and I would move into the smaller of the two bedrooms, giving the girls our larger one— a better use of space all around.

Emily didn't really share my level of enthusiasm. "Do not start that project today," she said. "You always think that a project is going to solve your problems. Please just relax."

I hate when people tell me to relax. But sometimes I have trouble sitting through an entire movie, so I knew she had a point. I was two days into leave from my job. The purpose of my leave was to rest and think about what I really wanted to do after I'd had an emotional meltdown on an NYC sidewalk a few months prior. The plan was also that I'd use the downtime to help care for our littlest girl at the time, Matilda.

"Please just relax while we're gone," she said again an hour or so later, turning and stepping out into the narrow hallway with our two girls and her sister, Audrey, who at the time was our downstairs neighbor.

I gave her a gentle, scheming smile.

As they walked down the hall, I closed the door and pressed my ear against it. I waited for the sound of their feet trudging down the three flights of stairs to the NYC sidewalks below.

Once the coast was clear, I started the move.

Seeing is believing. Show-and-tell had always been a hit with students in my classroom, and there was a reason for that. I knew that if I could actually show Emily the new arrangement, with the furniture swapped, she'd understand the greatness of my idea!

After preparing the girls' furniture for the swap—a crib, toddler bed, bookshelves, and wardrobes—and disassembling furniture in our bedroom, my plan hit a major snag. The furniture was too heavy for me to lift and move alone. I saw a pile of beach towels on the floor, grabbed them, and shimmied them underneath furniture legs so that I could slide the furniture while preventing damage to the floor. That was a good start, but it's not like it made the furniture any lighter. I had to resort to plan B. I feverishly emptied items out of dressers and wardrobes to make them lighter to move and quickly made piles all over the floor. I then realized I had completely obstructed my path.

It looked like all the pieces of furniture had thrown up. And then *I* wanted to throw up.

Piled before me were clothes and stacks of books, diapers, and blankets. I noticed parts of dehumidifiers, jewelry, and binders with notes from my graduate school classes. Photos, hair clips, hairbrushes, bows. Our disassembled queen-sized bed frame couldn't fit through the door, and it now lay in pieces halfway between the bedrooms.

I sat down for a moment and put my hands to my face. The chaos that surrounded me was a physical manifestation of the mental and emotional mess that I felt inside.

Click. I heard the lock turn. The blood drained from my face. I waded through the mess to the front door to intercept Emily.

"Please don't get mad," I said, which is never a good way to start a conversation. "I've been working on something that I want to show you."

Emily walked toward the bedrooms. Her face instantly flushed.

"You really did this?" she said in shock, walking from the first bedroom into the adjoining second room.

Audrey walked up behind her, gasped, and put her hand over her mouth.

The adoration and thanks that I had imagined would accompany this big reveal hadn't materialized. I'd anticipated an HGTV *Kiss and Cry* kind of reaction. In fact, the chaos I had created in that one hour took *months* for us to fully sort out.

Did you just flip over this book to confirm that the title is in fact *Tidy Up Your Life* and not *Mess Up Your Life*? I understand the confusion.

But stick with me, because this very messy story does have a much tidier ending.

Despite the chaos brought about by my hasty impulse to switch bedrooms, this episode was, thankfully, the start of a radical transformation in our home and in my life, one that would have a lasting impact far beyond the aesthetics and organization of our apartment.

My rash decision—plus the *months* of follow-up restoration it led to—triggered a project that would invite me to look hard at the mental and emotional messes that I'd hidden away for years and to unpack the professional and personal mess that had become my life. Tidiness, organization, and routines for managing a home and a life have followed. I can safely say I've learned a thing or two after causing our apartment to implode. This book is an effort to share those learnings with you so that your home won't implode, too.

But let me back up a bit. I think a proper introduction is in order. I'm Tyler. I'm a New York City teacher and now the father to *three* young daughters, Mabel, Matilda, and Margaret. Their three "M" names make labeling simple, but they sure are a tongue twister. I grew up in Kentucky; Emily and I met on the first day of eighth grade and got married shortly after graduating from college. She's forgiven me for my bedroom move plan and lots of other wild ideas over the years, and we've lived in New York City for almost fifteen years now.

As the opening scene of this book describes, clearly my life hasn't always been tidy—emotionally or physically! But I'm a dad who's been on a journey to tidy up my life. Hence my nickname, Tidy Dad.

In January 2019, I began to chronicle my tidying journey on Instagram, launching @tidydad after our local parenting groups began buzzing about a new show from Marie Kondo, the tidying extraordinaire, on Netflix. People were intrigued by some of Marie's concepts, but the overwhelming sentiment was "That's great but not realistic with kids." I set out to prove that a tidy space with kids was possible and that decluttering wasn't a one-and-done process. The same sister-in-law who witnessed the chaos that I'd created helped me put up my first post. It was a video tour of my tiny closet, which measures fourteen inches wide by seven feet tall. (Spoiler alert: That huge wardrobe that I'd put beach towels underneath to move didn't fit in the new smaller bedroom, so we had to let it go, along with many other things.)

On Instagram and our website and blog thetidydad.com, I've shared the systems and routines that Emily and I devised for our small space and our growing family, and my parallel journey to tidy up my professional life. I love showing how we've made life in our small apartment work for our family of five, and inspiring others to think creatively about how to declutter and make space for what's important in their own lives.

If you've picked up this book, your life might feel like a mess right now. There are probably dishes in the sink, laundry that needs to be folded. And you might be counting down the hours until you have to return to a job that feels like it is sucking all the mental and emotional energy from your life. You may just need to walk to the mirror right now and say "You're a mess," followed by "But you're going to be okay."

There are times when I've done that, and I always felt better.

But I'd like to invite you to embrace what I believe to be a more lasting strategy: the journey to tidy up your life. I've discovered that tidying is the deeply personal, emotional, and joyful process of bringing order to things. It's a process that transcends the aesthetics of our homes. It can be applied to our habits, routines, relationships, hobbies, and careers. You name it, you can learn to tidy it. Tidying is what has allowed me to make more space for the things that are truly important to me in life. I want the same for you.

How to Navigate This Book

Ernie from *Sesame Street* loves messes. For the rest of us, messes can feel incredibly overwhelming to tackle. This book will give you an entry point, a way to approach solving the problem. As I tell my students, the point is not to always be the fastest to find the solution, but rather to have the courage to get started and to be willing to continue trying until you reach the answer.

Toward that end, in the first part of this book, "Tidy Up Your Mind," we're going to unpack my key underlying strategies for tidying up all facets of your life. These strategies are drawn from my expertise as a teacher, Emily's expertise as a pediatric occupational therapist, and our journey to tidy up our physical space, and my life. There are five core strategies, and they run the gamut from headspace issues to decluttering your stuff to unpacking your baggage—emotional and physical! Because let's face it, if you consider your professional life to be a blazing success but your home is cluttered and disorganized and you're mentally and emotionally disconnected from your family, friends, and your feeling of self, life's still going to feel like a complete mess. Trust me— I've been there.

As any great daytime talk show promo does, I'll give you a snapshot of the "Tidy Up Your Mind" chapters:

Chapter 1 will help you unpack what's behind your mess. The alternate title to this chapter? Decluttering 101. Physical clutter is often a manifestation of the mental clutter we feel. Making sense of the mess and acknowledging the root causes is an important part of the decluttering process.

In chapter 2, I hope to get you thinking about your personal definition of "just enough." "Just enough" is the concept of choosing the amount in an individual category that is just right for you based on *your* current needs and season of life. It can apply to categories in the home like clothing, cookware, and toys, plus our personal and professional lives.

Next, in chapter 3, we're going to assess your rhythm and try to find a way to revamp your routines. The goal is to get a sense of the pattern of your life and activities within a period of time. The rhythms of life have a profound impact on how we allocate our time, resources, and energy. Routines help to simplify the intersection of all three allocations.

Chapter 4 is all about "Surthrival," which I define as intense periods of life when you have to do whatever it takes to survive, while also trying to thrive and not lose yourself in the process. Managing our homes, our careers, and our relationships looks different during these transitional and stressful seasons.

In chapter 5, I will help you stop doing all the work. Work happens both inside and outside of the home, and there are ways to apply strategic thinking to household tasks to make things feel a bit more manageable.

After tidying up our minds, in the second part of this book, "Tidy Up Your Space," we'll move on to the application of these concepts to the physical spaces in your home—from your bedroom and your kitchen to your hallway and your storage areas.

Whether you live in an apartment, a farmhouse in the country, or a castle in Europe (I actually have an Instagram follower who lives in a castle with multiple wings, and she has asked me to help her problem-solve how to stop losing her glasses!), there are ways that we can all tidy things up and design and organize spaces that work for us and not against us. We'll get into the nitty-gritty of physically organizing, tidying, and cleaning bathrooms, kitchens, living areas, bedrooms, and play areas. Our homes are sometimes like complex puzzles, and as Tidy Dad, I love figuring out creative solutions.

But the order matters! It's difficult to organize a space that hasn't been decluttered. It's difficult to tidy a space that isn't organized. And it's difficult to clean a space that isn't tidy. These distinct household activities build upon one another and are interrelated.

I want to help you declutter and create space in your life for the things that are important to *you*! After all, each of us has a different idea of what matters, of what's worth holding on to, storing away, or throwing out. Or, as I like to say, everyone's idea of "just enough" is unique. I can't dictate those measures for you, nor should anyone else, but I have developed ways to help you to define those measures for yourself. You can't upsize all areas of your life. You can't do it all, and you can't *keep it all*! It's time for you to define what's really important, and then to create the space to flourish.

Total change doesn't happen overnight. I remember staring at the piles I'd created during the Great Bedroom Flip and just wishing they'd go away, but there's value in sitting with the mess. I promise you that just by starting with the first few steps, you will feel lighter and calmer and be able to see a path that leads through the toys and the laundry basket to a tidier, happier, and simpler life. I know that your time is precious, and I'm grateful that you've picked up this book. The journey to tidy up your life starts now! Let's get to work!

PART ONE

TIDY UP
YOUR MIND

1

Unpack What's Behind Your Mess (Decluttering 101)

Physical clutter is often a manifestation of mental clutter. Whether you're trying to figure out the next step in your career or trying to figure out how to solve the mess that is your kitchen cabinet, probing what got you into the mess is the first step of the tidying process. It's difficult to make a path forward until you come to terms with what caused that mess in the first place.

Dean of Academics. What a fancy title, especially for a young former classroom teacher. It sounded impressive, particularly in NYC education circles, but don't be fooled. My job title should have been Dean of Mess, because that's really what I was. The "dean" title meant I was no longer a classroom teacher, no longer had summers off, and now had a lot of teacher management and student disciplinary responsibilities. That was difficult enough, but we'd also upsized our personal life. We had two kids under the age of two, and I was overwhelmed and exhausted.

So how did I get here?

Well, for years, everything moved along pretty much as I had planned. I checked off all the boxes on how I thought you're supposed to transition from your twenties to your thirties. Years earlier Emily and I had announced in Frank Sinatra style, "If I can make it there, I'm gonna make it anywhere. It's up to you, New York!" We'd made NYC our home, and now I was "successful." But this was all a façade. The only thing I'd really become successful at was crying in secret.

It always started as a burning sensation behind my eyes. Then my breathing became labored. My chin started to quiver as I held back tears. I'd wait until I'd kissed Emily and the girls goodbye and made it a few blocks from home on my two-mile walk to school. Then, as the tears threatened to spill out, I'd start to repeat a mantra that I'd taught to my former students: "I am kind, I am smart, I am going to have a great day no matter what!" Trouble was, for nearly three school years my days weren't that great. How bad? I'd characterize them as a dumpster fire.

Male elementary school teachers seem to have a shelf life of about five years in the classroom before people begin to ask questions, like "Why isn't he more ambitious?" and "Shouldn't he be an administrator by now?" My dad had been a teacher and followed an administrative track. He'd been an incredibly successful and well-respected elementary school principal and was able to balance his work with being a father to three kids. He was my role model. So, when I was offered a promotion to that fancy three-word title, I jumped at the opportunity.

Unfortunately, with my new position and two young children

at home, my life had become like an overstuffed closet—with way too many things precariously teetering behind closed doors, waiting for me to sort through them. In addition to navigating early parenthood and *all* the physical stuff that came with it, I'd also basically shoved all my stress, anxiety, and emotional baggage into the back of the closet (aka my mind) for that "someday" when I could process it all. Fatherhood had rewired my head and my heart, yet I felt like an impostor at work and at home. I would spend mornings, nights, and weekends trying to "catch up" on work, but could never seem to get ahead. I thought the logical way to solve problems at school was by working *more,* but it was just taking time away from my family. I felt like I wasn't good enough, strong enough, or competent enough to handle the stresses. But I dressed the part. While things may have looked tidy to others, I was experiencing a mental and emotional downward spiral.

One day, I stopped on the street on the way to school and had a complete breakdown. My chest tightened. My eyes darted from one side of the street to the other, watching the traffic pass. I could barely put one foot in front of the other. I took my phone from my pocket and called my wife. I told her I just couldn't keep going. I couldn't keep it all together anymore. I was honestly worried about what I might do to myself. I desperately needed help.

Confronting My Emotional Mess

I'd started to build the doors of my overstuffed closet—the tidy façade—back in the late '90s. I'd met Emily in eighth grade—her family had moved to Kentucky from Arkansas, and she had been assigned to sit next to me on the first day of school. That was one of the bright spots in an otherwise messy period of adolescence.

For starters, I was the target of schoolyard bullies. The Backstreet Boys shirt I'd worn on the first day of seventh grade had gotten things off on the wrong foot. I'd attended their concert with my sisters and best friend Jessie that summer, and apparently that wasn't a cool thing for a middle school boy to do. Then I made the mistake of telling on a group of kids who had been smoking in the back of the bus. They got in trouble, and I became their number one target. They verbally and physically harassed me for most of the year, to the point that I was scared to even use the bathroom at school.

On the bus, they'd throw chewed-up pieces of candy at me, broken pieces of glass, even full bottles of Gatorade. One afternoon we had a substitute bus driver, which gave the bullies the opportunity to unleash a whole new level of harassment. Someone hurled a D-size battery at me, striking me in the face. Twenty-five years later I have a permanent indentation on the side of my nose from the attack.

Then came the new century. I was very worried about the Y2K bug, a potential computer error that was supposedly going to cause computer systems around the world to crash. People feared ATMs would stop functioning, airplane navigation systems would stop working, and the power grids would shut down. Those fears never actualized; systems didn't implode. But what did implode in the new millennium was my parents' marriage. I hadn't seen that coming.

A "For Sale" sign went up in our front yard. The school bus driver noticed it and asked me excitedly where we were moving. I lowered my head and told him I didn't know. He probably thought we were just moving into a bigger house—a time-honored marker of moving on up—but the truth was that *I did* know what was happening: We were moving from one shared house into two.

Divorce may be commonplace now—and it wasn't unusual back then either—but I didn't have any friends whose parents were divorced, and I didn't personally know any divorced people, apart from my aunt and uncle, who had both been divorced before marrying each other. And in our southern, conservative Christian community, it was frowned on. I felt like I had a scarlet letter embroidered on all my clothing (though not on the Backstreet Boys shirt; I'd already donated that one). I felt embarrassed and ashamed.

To compensate and divert everyone's attention away from just being the "divorced kid," I tried to present myself as the best, the brightest, and the funniest. I graduated from high school with honors, was on the dean's list at college each semester, married Emily, became a teacher, and in my second year was named "Teacher of the Year" in my school and then in my entire district. I was accepted to a graduate school program at Columbia University, and Emily and I moved to New York City, where I planned to continue checking off the boxes of adulthood to prove that I was "successful."

I taught full-time and took night classes, and graduated with my master's degree in comparative and international education.

Doesn't that sound fancy? My grandpa, notoriously difficult to please, kept photos from my graduation in his wallet. He was impressed that I had attended an Ivy League school. For the first time in my life, I felt like I had made him proud. A few years later, accepting the promotion to Dean of Academics felt like more of the same—impressing others, making them proud, and presenting to the world the illusion that I had it all together.

If success meant working more hours, taking on more positional responsibility, and being "on call," then success had found me. Part of my new professional responsibility was to monitor students in crisis in our school's "recovery room," a place where they could cool down if they'd been demonstrating unsafe behaviors or tantruming in the classroom. I worked in tandem with one of our school social workers, Kim, the mother of two elementary school–aged children.

The work was emotionally and physically exhausting. We had a lot of students in crisis at school, and Kim and I were in the hot seat to help make things better. Kim provided the counseling to students, and I provided the suspension papers and met with parents and teachers. After one particularly tough morning—I was slapped across the face by a kindergartner at a meeting with him and his mother!—my façade was starting to crack. We all have a personal threshold for how much we can handle, and I'd reached my limit.

Kim saw me struggling, and she got real with me. "I'm a really good social worker, and everyone tells me that you were a really good teacher. *But what are you doing in this new job?* You're tired, completely worn down, and you have two young kids at home."

There was nothing secret about my crying at that point; I started to wipe tears from my eyes.

"Before I had my kids, I took every promotion," she continued. "Before I knew it, I was supervising a team of more than thirty social workers across Queens. By professional standards, I was *very* successful. But with each promotion I felt like I was getting further and further away from the work that I actually enjoyed doing. When I had my kids, I took some time off, and resolved to never be a manager again. I wanted to spend time doing work that I enjoyed and was really good at—working with kids, not supervising adults."

Kim was the first person I knew to forgo professional advancement. She'd wrestled with the thoughts of who she was versus who she wanted to be and had come to a decision. Her words struck me as revolutionary. I'd never met someone who'd intentionally given themself a demotion. I felt like my life was happening *to* me, yet it was clear that Kim had an acute sense of the type of professional work that she enjoyed and could articulate how her current position matched her personality, interests, and season of life. Her perspective really made me think.

To facilitate more of this "thinking," Emily and I had started couples therapy earlier in the fall. We were in crisis, and her sister, Audrey, had just been diagnosed with cancer. Emily and I were both spiraling. In our couples sessions, I dominated the conversation, which made me feel like I was "winning" at therapy. *Yay me!* Then one week our therapist, Suzanne, said, "Tyler, I think you could greatly benefit from individual sessions."

Afterward, while walking down the subway steps, I asked

Emily, "What do you think about Suzanne wanting me to start individual sessions? Do you think she thinks I'm the one with the issues in our relationship?"

"Maybe she just really enjoys your stories and wants to hear more about your life," Emily said with a laugh. "You're definitely a verbal processor. And also yes, clearly *you're* the one who needs more help."

She was being cheeky, but she was right. I was drowning in a sea of problems. The combination of the mental, physical, and emotional work I was doing felt crushing. For years I'd been suffering in silence. I just pushed on. "Never explain, never complain." Isn't that what Queen Elizabeth always said? Yet at this moment, what I cared most about was Suzanne liking me. Seeking the affirmation and approval of others was literally the story of my life.

I did move forward with individual therapy sessions, and spent time contemplating whether taking a leave from my job could be the next right move. The only time I'd ever "stepped back" before was during the Cupid Shuffle at wedding receptions. And let me tell you, I am great at that dance. But in life, stepping back had been much more difficult. Isn't it easier to just plow through? But look where that had gotten me.

Stepping back is the process of removing yourself from a situation so that you can assess and consider what might not be working. It's the process of identifying what you see, your role in what is happening, and how it makes you feel. Experience has now taught me that after you step back, you're able to consider ways to move forward. This is as true for big life decisions—like quality of life or work/life balance—as it is for reorganizing or decluttering your home.

In my first individual session with Suzanne, I casually mentioned that due to the recent passage of a new Paid Family Leave law in New York State, I had the opportunity to take parental leave and still bring in a percentage of my salary, because we had a child under the age of one at home. Well aware of how my anxiety was manifesting itself in my thoughts and behavior, she strongly endorsed the idea that I should take a leave from my job.

But I couldn't help feeling like an absolute failure. I had chosen to take the promotion, and I felt like it was up to me to figure out how to make it work. Suzanne challenged me to name what would happen if I *didn't* take the leave. I realized I couldn't keep going forward in this way. Although I feared what people might think of me, I decided to take the leave, and for a few months literally step back. I needed time and space to reassess my path.

Once the decision was made and I'd drafted my transition plan at school, it felt like I'd drawn a line in the sand. It was the first time that I'd ever chosen to prioritize my own well-being to that degree. I needed time and space to sort through the mess that my life had become. Not taking the time could have been catastrophic.

And given my mental state, I decided that two days into my leave was the perfect time to implode our apartment.

What a mess.

Confronting My Literal Mess

"At a bare minimum, we all need to have a place to sleep," Emily said, still assessing the mess that I'd created in our bedrooms.

Our temporary solution was to move the queen-sized bed into the smaller bedroom and put it lengthwise against the wall that had previously housed the toddler bed and crib. We then moved the crib and toddler bed into the larger bedroom.

As I closed my eyes on that first night in our new, smaller room, my thoughts raced with images of clutter piles, and I had a nightmare that I was being inexplicably attacked by pink tissue paper and couldn't breathe.

Apart from Emily's sister, Audrey, no one else knew of the chaos in our apartment. Have I mentioned that Audrey was also a social worker at my school? Talk about enmeshed. She knew *everything*.

To friends and family, it had probably looked like we had it all together, and our apartment had always appeared "tidy." But we'd become masters at hiding things away—physically and emotionally. And as we woke up the next morning, with our bed in the strangest location possible, we knew it was time to make a plan for confronting that situation.

Emily went to the library and checked out two books that we'd been wanting to read, *The Life-Changing Magic of Tidying Up* and *Spark Joy*, both by Marie Kondo. I believe that certain books enter our lives at just the right time, and Kondo's books helped provide us with a framework for how to confront the items in our home and make a plan for moving forward.

Asking Questions, in the Right Order

Whether you step back literally (from a punishing schedule or overwork) or emotionally (with or without your own Suzanne!), the process is liberating. Stepping back invites reflection and contemplation. The world could be a better place if more people did this. And I'm not just talking about applying this concept to your professional life. The concept can be applied to time, space, and resources.

Here are some questions to consider when stepping back:

☑ What am I observing right now?

☑ What do I see, hear, feel, and notice about my life?

☑ What about this makes it feel like a mess?

☑ How does the mess make me feel?

☑ How is this feeling rooted in core aspects of my identity?

☑ What do I really want? What do I really need?

☑ In what areas can I rely on myself?

☑ In what areas will I need to rely on others?

We learned that decluttering involves bringing everything out into the open, then carefully sorting, categorizing, and editing items, ultimately choosing which ones you want to take into your future. (Are you seeing the ways in which this applies to one's emotional life, too? Good, you're catching on! Also, *Thank you, Marie!*)

As we made our way from room to room, often shuffling large bins of items from place to place, we incorporated many of her principles, such as *Follow the right order,* and *Ask yourself if it "sparks joy"* (and let go of the rest).

Decluttering in the right order means that you work in a developmental progression. You start with items that are easier to sort and edit (which are not sentimental items!) and work toward progressively more difficult categories. Along the way, you hone your decision-making abilities, you learn things about yourself, and you determine what items you want to bring into your future. For Emily and me, this process of assessment and reflection helped us unearth some of the underlying feelings and emotions that we had about accumulating stuff.

Furthermore, we both had to ask ourselves what role we had played in the creation of the mess. That helped us begin to unpack the emotional reasons clutter formed in the first place. And our reflections helped us make a plan for moving forward.

It's emotionally overwhelming to empty a cabinet, drawer, closet, or wardrobe and to consider the role that *you* played in amassing the clutter you find there. It's natural to feel a mix of embarrassment and regret. Excess feels incredibly wasteful. Allowing yourself to sit with those uncomfortable feelings is a powerful part of the "tidy up your life" process. The goal is to identify the root cause of the problem, put steps in place to address the problem, and then prevent the problem from happening again.

For us, the plan included clearing all our spaces, gathering items in a central location, and sorting items into categories *before* choosing what to keep, what to move out, and how to organize things. We emptied closets, my wardrobe, and nightstands. In the process, we discovered some *questionable* things—like my wisdom teeth. Yes, you just read that correctly! My wisdom teeth, which had been removed many years earlier, had somehow survived the move from my high school bedroom, to our first apartment in Kentucky, to our first apartment in New York City, and to our current apartment. Why? In what world would those ever be useful again?!

Believe me, we had a lot to let go of.

Reassessing the Hypothetical Someday

How many casserole dishes do you currently have in your kitchen, for the hypothetical someday when you need to deliver casseroles to three separate friends who are all recovering from surgery at the same time?

How many cellphone chargers do you have, for the hypothetical someday when fifteen friends come over to your apartment, all with dead cellphone batteries?

And how many socks are currently in your sock drawer, for the hypothetical someday when all your socks are in the dirty clothes hamper, and you really want to go for a run in a fresh pair of socks?

The internal dialogue for holding on to an item can sound like this:

> *"I really should hold on to ____, just in case ____ happens."*
>
> *"If ____ happens, then it would be good to have ____!"*
>
> *"I know my kids are only ____, but my grandkids might love playing with ____ too."*
>
> *"If I get rid of ____, what'll happen when ____?"*

This dialogue isn't inherently problematic, but the hypothetical someday can become a major point of tension when decluttering. I mean for years, I'd been reflecting on my work life with a similar lens, saying on repeat, *"When____happens, things'll be so much better."*

That line of thinking and questioning can invite us to hold on to, and dare I say, hoard items long after they're needed, functional, or serving us in our current life stage. It's important to recognize when those narratives start to surface and to interrogate *why* the thoughts are happening and *where* the thoughts are coming from.

As we cleared spaces and then sorted and categorized items in our apartment, we had to confront our feelings around planning for the hypothetical someday. When we became parents to our first child, it had been relatively easy to set up organization systems for all the *stuff* that seems to come with a baby. We'd both studied childhood development, and we had all the appropriate toys, all the baby gear, all the energy.

Anticipating a second child someday, we stored everything Mabel had outgrown for that someday to come. But once Matilda arrived our level of exhaustion seemed to compound—as did the stuff—and things got messy.

I'd upsized my responsibilities at school, we'd upsized the number of people who lived in our apartment, and we didn't have clear systems for the mountain of hand-me-downs and the increasing number of toys or consistent routines for how to manage our life. And did I mention that we were exhausted?

And then came a barrage of more hypothetical someday questions asked of us, and that we asked ourselves: "Is New York City where we want to raise our children long-term?" and "Do we want to have a third child?" and "Is this apartment going to become too small?"

Do you ever just want to scream, "SHUT UP!" when you're on the receiving end of hypothetical questions?

I know it's not a kind phrase, but for me, the answer is yes. Sometimes it feels like *everyone* has questions, and I've come to learn that you don't always have to answer them.

As we began to sort, make piles, and declutter our lives, Emily and I silenced those hypothetical someday questions and resolved to embrace the now. Because what was the alternative? Give up our life in NYC and cave to how others suggested we live our life? We tried to name for ourselves what we needed for this current season and we worked together as a team to make sense of the mess.

It was difficult work, but to the best of our abilities, we withheld our judgments of each other, refusing to place sole blame on the other for the volume of items that had accumulated. For months, we had decluttering parties after the girls went to bed. As much as we wanted to quickly sort through things, throw them behind closed doors again, and move on with our lives, we had to force ourselves to learn how to step back, be still, and consider how to make a path forward. New York City was our home. Stuffing things away was no longer an option.

We grow and change, our children grow and change, and so we have to revisit our efforts to declutter and prune away what we don't need (or don't need now) continually.

Five years after our epic decluttering party—I'm calling it a party, because it involved late nights, some music, some laughter, some tears, and a few cocktails—we've learned that decluttering is a continual process. Our lives aren't stagnant. We grow and change, our children grow and change, and so we have to revisit our efforts to declutter and prune away what we don't need (or don't need now) continually. And we've learned how to apply the principles of decluttering to other, higher-stakes questions about our personal and professional lives.

Decluttering 101

The first step to tidying up your life is to get clear on the *why* behind the accumulation of all your stuff—physical, mental, and emotional. Again, that's not a quick fix. It can take time to gain the perspective you may have been lacking. In the meantime, however, let's get specific about what it'll take to literally start to unpack your "stuff."

Like anything that takes practice, decluttering gets so much easier with time. Curbing the influx of new things into your space helps, too. I know that's easier said than done, but I promise—it's something you can get better at! If you want to get started decluttering something in your life—work, relationships, your sock drawer—use my hard-earned advice. Here's the decluttering cycle that I recommend:

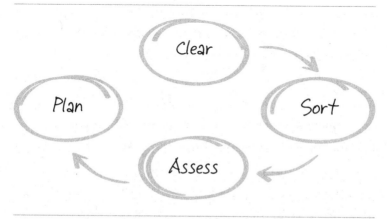

Decluttering Cycle

Clear

Sort

Assess

Plan

Decluttering boils down to four things: clearing the space, sorting items, assessing what you see, and then making a plan for the items you want to keep. Decluttering takes time, intentionality, and personal reflection. The most powerful part of the process is determining what contributed to the mess in the first place. You also have to declutter with the belief that things are going to get better. Because they will.

Scheduled Decluttering

"It seems like you all are always unloading some closet and going through stuff," I remember my brother-in-law Braden saying, years before he had kids of his own. "Is this like your hobby or something?"

"Less of a hobby, more of a reality," I said.

Indeed, our space is an ever-evolving puzzle. As the girls grow and their needs change, our apartment must adapt and change with them. Unless of course we just pack up the things in our apartment and move to the Midwest. (I'm foreshadowing things to come here, not for us, but for Braden.) We believe that "home" is primarily a space for our family to live life, not store stuff, so decluttering is not a one-and-done thing. We don't have an attic or basement or garage to store away items, and I'm kind of grateful for that. We're continually forced to confront the number of physical items that we have in our home.

Over time, we have established a *schedule* for intensive decluttering projects (and for decluttering breaks). I think of this as decluttering with intention, as opposed to decluttering after an implosion—been there, done that. Decluttering with intention sounds like "The holidays are coming up—we should think about what toys the girls are ready to move out and make space for new things to come in." That sounds very different from "There's so much stuff in here. It's ridiculous how many toys they have. They never play with any of them. These are all getting donated!"

Decluttering with intention allows you to work in sync with a coming season and to move out items during a period of time when *other* people are on the hunt for those types of used items—shout-outs to my local Buy Nothing group and Preloved groups. Half the battle with decluttering is going through things and making decisions. The other half is actually getting the stuff out of your space. You want to think strategically about when to declutter, with the consumer in mind. People aren't looking for winter coats for their kids in June, but they certainly are in October!

Using the calendar on the following page as a guide, create your own list of the areas that need to be regularly decluttered in your home. Don't just copy ours; if you have a garage, attic, basement, yard, or additional rooms in your home, you'll want to include those, too! Remember, decluttering isn't a onetime event, and having a schedule helps to free up important mental space—when you know you've set a time that you'll "get to that stuff," you don't have to worry about it so much right *now.*

Decluttering Calendar

January

- ☑ Papers (tax prep)
- ☑ Kitchen and pantry
- ☑ Household back stock

February

- ☑ Spring clothing
- ☑ Spring gear
- ☑ Travel gear/bags

March

- ☑ Great Toy Edit, part 1
- ☑ Bedrooms
- ☑ Wardrobe/closets

April

- ☑ Bathroom/toiletries
- ☑ Travel activities
- ☑ Tech gear

May

- ☑ Summer clothing
- ☑ Summer gear
- ☑ Swim supplies

June

- ☑ School papers
- ☑ Outdoor play items
- ☑ Car supplies

July

Decluttering break

August

- ☑ Fall clothing
- ☑ Fall gear
- ☑ School supplies

September

- ☑ Shared living areas
- ☑ Dress-up clothing
- ☑ Art supplies

October

- ☑ Winter clothing
- ☑ Winter gear
- ☑ Holiday decor

November

- ☑ Great Toy Edit, part 2
- ☑ Baking/party items
- ☑ Entryway

December

Decluttering break

INDEPENDENT PRACTICE

Embrace the Power of a Ten-Minute Declutter

Are you ready to unlock the transformative power of just ten minutes? Choose a specific area in your home or workspace that is a mess (but for this exercise, please don't choose to switch bedrooms with your kids!). It could be the kitchen counter, your nightstand, the top of your dresser, your work bag. Choose an area that you can realistically tackle in ten minutes or less.

Completely *clear* the area and *sort* items by category. Then *assess* items and consider what to keep, discard/donate, or rehome in a new location. Next the fun part: Develop a *plan* for how to organize items and place essential and useful items back in the designated area.

Then reflect: How did the process feel? The goal of this practice is to quickly assess and declutter a small area by testing each item's usefulness and importance. And it's also to train your brain to take advantage of the power of focused, ten-minute work bursts. You're busy, and decluttering takes time. But ten-minute decluttering sessions can help you flex your decluttering muscles and gradually help you gain control over your space.

2

Define "Just Enough" for You

The goal of tidying is to make space for what's really important . . . *to you*. There's power in being able to name and make the necessary space for your priorities. Once you can articulate what "just enough" means in the categories of your life, you can begin to flourish.

We'd transitioned from the shock and chaos stage of our Great Bedroom Flip to the practical "How are we going to make this work?" phase.

"We have two options that I see," I said to Emily. "We can put the wardrobe in front of the window. It blocks the light that way, but we just sleep in here anyway. Or we get rid of the wardrobe, and we share a closet?"

"We can't block the window with a wardrobe!" Emily said. "But I also don't want to share my new closet. I finally made everything fit."

For years, Emily had a closet *and* a dresser, and I had used a wardrobe. Now she had successfully edited her clothing down to be able to move the dresser inside the closet in our new room, giving her a combination of folded space and hanging space.

"There's also that tiny closet over there," I said, pointing to the far corner of the room. Our landlords had constructed a narrow floor-to-ceiling closet around the bedroom door, and we'd been using the tiny closet as a makeshift "catchall" area. Practical, yes. Functional, no.

"So," I continued, "if I got rid of some more of my stuff, we could move the wardrobe back into the larger bedroom to reconfigure for the girls, and I could use that tiny corner closet?"

Judging from Emily's expression (and the doghouse I was in for having created the mess in the first place), I knew this was her preferred solution.

I began clearing out items from the small closet. For many people, their guest bedroom is the catchall room; this closet was ours. I heaped pillows, kitchen items, extra pairs of shoes, holiday decor, and sentimental items like mementos from our wedding onto the floor.

Pro Tip

I find that when I'm faced with a big pile of *stuff*, it can be psychologically easier to deal with by scanning for what I love and want to keep. Picking up each of those things and taking the time to remember why I saved them in the first place is a happy exercise! What's left is what can be donated or thrown away.

Taking deep breaths, we assessed the overwhelming pile and identified what we really wanted to keep, which felt like a more positive foot forward than starting with what to toss or give away. Then we moved the pile of items into the small playroom adjoining the bedrooms. This became our staging area, our makeshift "find this stuff a permanent home" room.

Next, I unloaded the wardrobe. The test was on. Could I reduce my clothing to fit in the tiny closet? I piled everything onto the bed and sorted items into individual categories. As I assessed the situation, and the mess, I realized that a lot of my clothes were repeats (So. Many. Blue. Plaid. Shirts!) and that given the logistical constraints of my new closet and my motivation to make it work, a major edit was needed. I first looked for the items I really loved and felt sure I wanted to keep.

Let's be real: I'm definitely not a flashy dresser. I've always been drawn to simple looks concentrated around the core color that makes me happy: navy blue. But how many blue shirts does one person need? As I sorted items and chose what to keep, I started to create combinations of outfits and realized that my favorites were those that were easiest to match and coordinate with the other items that were blue, olive green, burgundy, and tan. I had other clothing in colors that weren't those four, but I began to see them as outliers.

I also looked for items that had a more breathable, athletic fit and were made of fabrics that support my active lifestyle—I walk two miles each way to and from school, so that's twenty miles per week of walking in my work clothes. Also, because I'm not a fan of ironing, I got rid of anything prone to wrinkles.

It felt liberating to name my favorite qualities of each piece of clothing and to force myself to provide a rationale for why I wanted to keep it.

The result of my editing efforts was a "capsule wardrobe." I had no room for excess, but I realized that I still had just enough clothing. I organized the clothing I chose to keep into nice vertical folds and arranged items by color. It continues to feel nice *not* to share a closet or dresser, or to need to ask for Emily's input during future clothing edits (which I continue to do seasonally). My tiny closet is a physical representation of my personal ability to choose and set boundaries on my own physical possessions, and it feels wonderful to have exactly what I need, arranged exactly as I like. It's my "small but mighty" solo space. It just happens to be only fourteen inches wide, but it's made all the difference in my life.

There's No Need to Get All Minimalist

I want to be clear about one thing here, though. While I was able to fit all my clothing into a fourteen-inch-wide closet, I don't consider myself to be a minimalist—my eclectic swimwear and pajama set collections make that clear—although I do appreciate and practice many aspects of the philosophy. I define minimalism as the practice of intentionally reducing the number of items in your home to the bare minimum. It's about eliminating all unnecessary possessions, with the goal of achieving more clarity, efficiency, and contentment through deliberate simplification and prioritization.

Minimalism works for some people—it can make them feel lighter and freer. It also makes for a beautiful magazine spread—very little on tables, no clutter, lots of empty, dust-free surfaces! But I admit that focusing on maintaining the minimum number of items in a space can feel defeating and at times unrealistic.

Sometimes when you just remove, remove, remove, you're left with space that feels empty or barren. That's not my goal with tidying. My goal is to make more space for what's really important. That's where the "just enough" concept comes in.

"Just enough" means having what is necessary to meet a person's or family's needs at that stage of life, without all the excess. It involves the process of editing, but it's not about trying to reduce things to the lowest possible number. Saying "no" to items in one category can open up space for items in another. You can choose to make room for your interests, hobbies, and priorities to flourish. For instance, if you're an avid skier, then you need to make space for your skis!

Testing out your personal definition of "just enough" with physical objects can be an incredibly helpful place to start. After solving the problem of my closet, we moved on to another category of items: TOYS. Oh, the toys.

"Why do we have five different block sets?" I asked in the midst of a tidying frenzy.

"Because they're all different," Emily answered.

"They're all blocks. Choose one set," I said, freshly inspired by my success with editing clothing. "I'm donating the rest!"

As I quickly learned, however, different block sets really do serve different purposes. Did you know that stacking and balancing wooden blocks on top of one another requires fine motor skills that are different from those needed to push together interlocking blocks or to connect magnet blocks? Emily knew this because of her experience as an occupational therapist, so she wanted to keep what we had. In order to make more space for the blocks, she was willing to donate several of our large baby/toddler toys that served only one purpose. It was not that Emily was trying to keep everything, but she had different priorities about what stayed and what went.

So why have five block sets when we could probably get by with only one? Because we're not minimalists. We can choose to keep items that support our interests and our kids' interests in a specific season of life. It was important to Emily, and ultimately to me, to have quality open-ended toys that allow our girls to be creative, inquisitive, and imaginative.

I've made peace with the fact that for years to come, we'll have a steady flow of new items into and out of our home based on the changing developmental needs and interests of our children. We've set boundaries and made choices in order to make space for the block sets . . . and art supplies . . . and dress-up items . . . and the list keeps going. Right now, our girls' favorite is baby dolls, but in a few years it'll be something else. Whatever it is we find ourselves accumulating, we'll have to make space for those items by regularly decluttering and considering what is needed for the current season. An extreme focus on the number of items that are in our apartment at any given time would feel overwhelming. Remember, the goal isn't just to remove, remove, remove, but to make space for what really matters to you. For my older sister, Amanda, that's a collection of dozens of foam fingers. My mom is a prolific paint-by-numbers enthusiast and has a lot of large-scale prints hanging in her home. My dad collects and displays model cars. My younger sister, Kristin, owns dozens of farm animals. Her husband has over seventy pairs of pants in his closet. To each their own!

"Just enough" decisions can also move beyond the physical

possessions in our homes. This concept can be applied to other categories such as habits, careers, finances, relationships, and how you spend your time.

Ditching a Hermit Crab Mentality

Emily and I have lived on the same street in New York City for more than a dozen years, in two different apartments. The first one was a cozy little five-hundred-square-foot one-bedroom, but we shared the building with our landlords—a brother-and-sister pair—who seemed annoyed that we lived in *their* home, even though they were the ones who had rented the downstairs apartment to us. They'd pull back their curtains to watch us every time we left the building, and when we returned they would peek down at us in the hallway from their upstairs door. We wondered if they were retired CIA operatives. As soon as we could, we broke that lease and moved into our current two-bedroom railroad-style apartment, where we have brought all three girls home.

There are lots of reasons to love this apartment. It's close to school, close to the subway, and close to the barbershop where the girls color or read while I get my haircut. The playground is a block away, the library and post office are nearby, we have a Laundromat and a grocery store just around the corner, there are plenty of restaurants and bakeries, and we're able to walk almost everywhere we want to go. With the girls in the larger bedroom now, things feel manageable. Life in NYC feels simple.

Another factor that made our living arrangement ideal for

years was our proximity to family. For eight years, Emily's sister, her husband, and their kids lived in the same building as us. Between our two families we welcomed home five babies. My brother-in-law Braden was Mabel's first nanny. We babysat for each other, hosted lots of cousin sleepovers, and loved the fact that we could run downstairs or they could run upstairs if someone ran out of a necessity like baby wipes, dish soap, or another random item in the midst of a perceived emergency. For a season, we even shared dinner responsibilities. We'd trade off nights and cook a double batch of food, then drop it off at the other family's apartment.

Living this way—in a kind of mini family compound—made us the envy of many friends. This built-in support system even inspired newspaper stories in both *The New York Times* and the *New York Post*!

But after years together, Audrey and Braden decided to move to Indiana, and—incidentally—into a home that was four times the size of our identical apartments! We always knew that our family compound might not last forever, but it was a shock to our family system anyway when it came to pass. It made Emily and me question whether we should trade spaces, too. And I don't mean trade spaces with our neighbors and make over one room in our home with the help of a designer and $1,000 (shout-out to TLC's *Trading Spaces*—one of my guilty pleasures back in the early 2000s!). I mean pack up all our possessions and move into a larger space, because after all, American culture always tells us bigger is better.

When I find myself playing the "comparison game," I remind

myself of the humble hermit crabs that our parents allowed my sisters to bring home from the beach when we were little kids. I thought they smelled bad, and I didn't like wildlife living in and crawling around our home, but my aversion aside, I see parallels between those little crustaceans and the American way of life.

Hermit crabs grow to fit the size of their shell, and then they shed that shell and look for a larger one. This is very similar to what culture tells us humans about the square footage of our homes: that as our families grow, we should make more money, we should acquire more possessions, and we should look for a larger space to live. And we've internalized this mentality! I mean, when we moved from our five-hundred-square-foot apartment to the new apartment, it felt like a palace, but fast-forward a few years and it began to feel cramped. That's when the decluttering parties kicked in.

Here's the truth: More square footage doesn't mean that there's less of a mess, it just means that your mess may be less concentrated. Many people who live in spaces much larger than ours have told me that in some ways their larger space can exacerbate things and make it feel like the mess is *even more spread out*! Plus, they have so many more spaces in which to hide things away.

So even though our definition of "home" doesn't fit with everyone's definition, we've made the decision to stop keeping up with the Joneses. Who are the Joneses anyway?

Over the years, we have looked into the option of moving into a larger apartment or a newer building, but each time we determined we would rather save for a future home purchase, investments, travel, education, or experiences, rather than significantly

Trading Up or Trading Within?

Congratulations are typically given when someone decides to move into a larger home, whereas choosing to stay in a smaller space long-term often invites questions and critiques. While trading spaces can sometimes be a good move, it can also be easy to buy more stuff, run out of room, need more square footage, then need more money, have to work more hours, and then realize it's all taking time away from what matters to you. There can be freedom in making the decision to evolve instead of trade. That's something to celebrate, too!

Here are some important questions to consider when wrestling with the question of "Do we need to change spaces, or does our space need to change?"

☑ What needs does our family have for this current season of life?

☑ How do we allocate space in our home to meet those needs?

☑ What are the top priorities of our family right now?

☑ Are there any priorities that are in competition with one another?

☑ How could we creatively evolve our space to match our priorities?

increase the cost of our rent. Over and over, we have come to the conclusion that we don't need more square footage.

We've learned that you don't always need to change spaces, but that your space will need to change. Multiple times, we've made big changes—we've completely reconfigured closets and changed the function of rooms. We've also made small adjustments, like moving a crib to a different side of the room so our neighbor would stop banging on the wall when one of our babies was crying. The process of evolving can breathe new life into a space and, at least for now, we are comfortable knowing the amount of space we have is *just enough* for our current season of life.

The Domino Effect

Switching bedrooms has helped us to embrace the power of a domino effect. Implementing small adjustments to our living space led to adjusted routines, which led to our feeling like this space could work for not just two kids, but eventually three! We also got some clarity on other priorities, including my deciding to take a pay cut and return to teaching. I briefly considered leaving the education profession entirely or switching schools, but as my parental leave came to an end, I started to formulate my plan to return to the classroom at the same school where I'd been the Dean of Academics. I took a page from my own playbook and started to declutter my work life. I knew I needed to step back professionally for the sake of my mental health and my family, but starting over completely felt too overwhelming.

I had no model for navigating the process of stepping back. I didn't know anyone who'd ever asked their employer for a demotion! I had so many hypothetical questions: "Would the teaching staff accept me back as one of their own?" and "How would I explain this demotion someday in a job interview?" Just as I'd done with our physical possessions, I had to ditch those types of questions. For the first time, I put my family and myself first and made a decision that wasn't based on what others would think of me. The judgment and critique I feared would come from others didn't arise. Sure, I took a pay cut, and my ego took a hit when I explained my decision to friends and colleagues, but it was also a major turning point in my life. I learned that sometimes you have to step back in order to move forward.

As I shared my decision with my principal, I envisioned my future self commuting to and from school with the girls. I knew that in the blink of an eye, my daughters would be school age and they'd be able to attend the school where I worked. It wasn't just the commuting time that I looked forward to, it was realizing that I'd personally know their teachers and have a kind of connection to the girls that I'd never have had if I worked at a different school or took a different job.

Moral of the story? There is no shame in taking the easiest, least complicated route. In certain seasons, it's the *best* route.

The next fall I organized and set up my new classroom, was introduced to my new co-teacher (who became one of my best friends), and felt an overwhelming sense of renewed balance. My new professional responsibilities felt like *just enough* and opened up time and space for Emily and me to breathe a little bit, and even dream. Stepping down from my administrative job gave me the gift of summers off with my family, which led us to try to answer the question of how and where we would spend them together.

Sometimes you have to step back in order to move forward. . . . There is no shame in taking the easiest, least complicated route. In certain seasons, it's the *best* route.

For years, "owning an Airbnb" had been on our bucket list, and each time we rented a place outside of the city, Emily and I talked about how fun—and what a great investment it would be—to own and run one ourselves. By September 2019—months before the pandemic would make us truly stir-crazy—we had an overwhelming urge to start looking for a place. We loved New York City, but finding a larger space a few hours outside the city where we could host family was becoming increasingly important to us. Emily was pregnant with our third child, and we wanted a space where we could comfortably host our parents for visits.

I love "shopping" on Zillow, and we started exploring options within about two hours of New York City, where we could invest in a rental property. Over Labor Day weekend we drove to a quaint town in the Poconos of Pennsylvania, and looked at three houses with a real estate agent named Russell. Refreshingly, he put *zero* pressure on us to buy. In fact, he tried to talk us out of putting an offer on our favorite house, because he deemed it "too small" for our family. We assured him the eleven hundred square feet would be *just enough* for us.

"Most people want the most square footage at the max of their price budget," Russell said. "But it seems like you all want the opposite."

"I guess so," I said with a laugh. "But we want to make sure this home is something that we can afford each month in addition to our apartment, without being dependent on the rental income. We don't want to get in over our heads."

"That's actually smart," Russell said. "A smaller house also means lower property taxes and less to maintain."

In the end, we made an offer on the little cottage. Built in 1974, it had been completely renovated by the previous owner. It felt "right" to us—it was just enough space to house us and friends or family on weekends when we weren't renting it out, and also just enough space to accommodate us for full-time living in the summers.

Now, I know what you might be thinking. "Tidy Dad, you've just told me to establish what is just enough, yet you don't just have one living space, but TWO?!"

I acknowledge that our living arrangement—renting an apartment in New York City and owning a cottage in Pennsylvania—is a bit unique, but again, that's the beauty of establishing a personal definition of what is just enough. Deciding what's just enough means you are able to establish the categories that you care about versus those that aren't as important.

For us, purchasing the cottage was never about acquiring "more" in the literal sense. It was about creating the mental, emotional, and physical space for time and connection with our families. It was about having a space for adventure, retreat, and joy. This arrangement has given us the best of both worlds—city life during the school year, and mountain life in the summertime. Our trusty 2000 Chevy Malibu shuttles us seamlessly between those two worlds.

INDEPENDENT PRACTICE

Define What Is "Just Enough" for You

Living with "just enough" is not about making drastic changes or living a bare-minimum existence, it's about naming for yourself what's important and finding balance between your possessions, your space, and your life.

I invite you to begin to craft your personal definition of "just enough" and start to interrogate how you are currently living in alignment with that definition. It may be helpful to grab a journal, a piece of paper, or open the Notes app on your phone and actually write out your own definition of "just enough." This is deeply personal work, and I want you to keep the following categories in mind.

1. **Consider the current situation:** Take a moment to think about your current living situation and lifestyle. Consider your living space, possessions, daily routines, and activi-

ties. Are there areas where you feel overwhelmed by excess or where you could simplify?

2. **Reflect on influences:** Think about factors that have shaped your outlook on life. These could include upbringing, cultural influences, societal norms, personal experiences, or values instilled by family or friends or self.

3. **Identify assumptions:** Examine any assumptions or beliefs you hold about what constitutes "enough" in various areas of your life. Are these assumptions based on necessity, societal expectations, personal desires, or other factors?

4. **Define "just enough":** Think about what "just enough" means to you. It could include having the essentials without excess, or living within or below your means. Write down a definition that captures your interpretation of this concept.

3

Find Your Rhythm and Make It Routine

You have more control than you might think! You are in charge of how you run your home and how you run your life. You're able to set boundaries around time, energy, and resources. You may just need some practice. You are the conductor of the symphony of your life. It's time to name your rhythms and harness the power of routines.

Routines are there to serve you, not control you. It can be helpful to consider why routines in your life are currently happening or unfolding the way they are. There's power in staying curious about difficult rhythms and taking time to ask yourself "What's underneath this little hiccup or issue?" Then you can consider what's within your power to fix.

On the first day in my new classroom with my new co-teacher, I knew that we were kindred spirits and were going to be a dynamic team. Kierra, a seasoned teacher from California, had recently moved to New York City with her husband, an aspiring filmmaker. Kierra was on her second act of sorts. She'd been a makeup artist in Hollywood, working on film sets for years, before going back to school to get her teaching credential. Now she was ready to "simplify her life," as she and her husband were looking forward to having children, saving for a "bougie" little chicken farm somewhere in the tristate area, and trying to figure out what came next.

I could relate to Kierra's story in a lot of ways. I'd tidied up the implosion of my career path, and was also trying to navigate a season of "what's next." But for the first time I wasn't anxious about the "what's next," and neither was Kierra. It was refreshing to work with someone who was unpretentious, funny, and thoughtful. I looked forward to coming to work every day. We ran our classroom like cohosts on a daytime talk show. But the best part was that the audience couldn't change the channel—they were forced to be there.

I love being a teacher. Stepping back into the classroom narrowed my workplace responsibilities and lifted the mental and emotional fog that had completely surrounded me during those administrative years. It brought back a healthy routine to my life.

I thrive on routine. And I fundamentally believe that children do, too. And when you find your rhythm, when you're able to concretely come to terms with the season of life that you're in, you can develop routines that not only solve problems, but bring a little joy to your life. In this chapter I'm going to pull back the curtain on some of the routines that are working for me and our family, and also introduce some frameworks that can be applied to your family as well.

Routine Joy

I look forward to my walks to and from school with the girls, come rain, shine, or snow. Each day, we pass our "friends": the man who sprinkles birdseed for the pigeons at the same street corner, at the same time, each morning; the lady in a motorized wheelchair with a parrot on her shoulder. (Yes, you read that correctly.) In a city as large and diverse as New York, the rhythm of our commute and the regular characters in our story are comforting—familiar signposts.

But commuting four miles each day round-trip, me on foot and the girls on scooters beside me, is no small feat. To celebrate the end of five days of learning and commuting back and forth to school, we've instituted "Foodie Friday," an age-appropriate and relatively risk-free way (apart from the time when they *each* ordered $18 milkshakes) for me to hand over some control to the girls and let them choose a treat for Friday afternoon. During the school week they don't have a choice over what they wear to school (thank goodness for uniforms!), what time they go to bed, what time they wake up, or what they have for dinner. I enjoy handing over control on Foodie Fridays.

This simple rhythm to the week and the Foodie Friday routine have become predictable parts of the week and bring a considerable amount of joy to us all. As they should! The best routines are ones that you fall into happily and that provide comfort and support in your day or week.

It's possible to create routines for varying aspects of life that do this for you, but you have to be intentional and strategic about developing them. This can take some experimentation—sometimes a routine that you want very much to institute for yourself (go to the gym three days a week after work!) or for your family (everyone under the age of ten in bed by 7 P.M.) doesn't "stick." That's frustrating, but it's something I can help you troubleshoot.

Hearing the Rhythm of Your Life

My daughters love music and are fortunate to have talented music teachers (shout-out to Ms. Howell) at their school. Borrowing a metaphor from music, I can acknowledge that some seasons of my life have felt like a symphony, while others have felt like the strings, the woodwinds, and the brass are playing at different tempos, creating a cacophony of sounds clashing together. Is my life *now* perfectly tidy? Absolutely not, but I feel better equipped to handle the noise. I'm learning that in difficult seasons, I don't necessarily have to throw out an entire instrument or banish a section from the orchestra. Sticking with this metaphor, I just need to pull out the metronome to listen, set the rhythm that I need, and then adjust to the beat.

Emily and I consider ourselves to be co-conductors of our family's life symphony. We are also planners by nature and as we discussed when to have a third child, Mabel's anticipated school schedule was top of mind. A five-year age gap between our oldest and youngest would mean that Emily would be home with two

How Life Is Like a Symphony

Conducting Your Symphony: You are the conductor of your life symphony. The choices you make when orchestrating the various components can create a harmonious and balanced experience . . . or not. Your personal life, work life, and family life all interact with one another to create the song of your life. The musical repertoire and routines you select for each season of life will ebb and flow.

Sections and Movements: Life can be divided into sections or movements, each representing a specific aspect such as college, dating, early parenthood, middle parenthood, retirement, caring for aging parents, and more. Each section contributes its unique melody to the symphony, and it's important to recognize what section you're in.

Tempo and Dynamics: Each movement will have a different pace. Some may be fast-paced and energetic, while others are slow and contemplative. It's important to adjust your schedules, routines, and priorities to the demands of each section.

Harmony and Balance: It's important to strive for harmony and balance in your symphony. As conductor, you have to ensure that no single instrument (or aspect of life) dominates the composition. Each element should complement and enhance the overall experience.

Solo Performances: Allow for solo performances, and give yourself permission to experience individual choice time. This could look like going for a run, reading a book, or taking a fun class. It's beautiful to experience life with others, but solo time is incredibly valuable, too.

Improvisation: Life is unpredictable, and you'll need to be open to spontaneity and change and be willing to pivot. It's like jazz! Embrace the unexpected notes; they'll add richness and depth to your symphony or invite you to learn or realize something new.

Intermissions and Rests: Recognize the importance of intermissions and rests. Just as a musical piece needs pauses for balance, your life benefits from moments of reflection, relaxation, and rejuvenation. Book a massage, sit on the couch and read a book, take a nap, write in your journal, order takeout for dinner, and give yourself permission to not be productive for a designated period of time.

kids once Mabel went to kindergarten. That rhythm felt manageable.

But then baby Margaret made her entrance on the world stage the *same* day that New York City shut down because of the COVID pandemic. That certainly had an impact on our family rhythms. In a way, all the world's collective symphonies fell silent.

Mabel attended kindergarten remotely the entire next school year while we had a toddler and a newborn at home. I taught remotely from a closet at our cottage, and like everyone else we were isolated physically from our friends and family.

Like most people around the world during that time, we did whatever we could to stave off our fears. We were totally in what I call "surthrival mode" (see chapter 4). In our case, we had family dance-offs at night. For a few moments the weight of the world was lifted off our shoulders and we just smiled and danced—not well, of course, but happily.

Post-pandemic, our weekday rhythms are much more structured and predictable(ish). I walk the older two girls to school and Emily walks Margaret to preschool. We're all home together in the afternoons, and we have a bit of playtime, or what we call "choice time," before the evening shuffle begins. We eat dinner together, transition the girls through baths, pajamas, brushing teeth, and reading books, and put them to bed, and then the cycle repeats again the next day. We've considered extracurricular activities, but right now, this feels like *just enough* for us.

On school year weekends, we've tried to create rhythms of adventure, rest, and play. In the summer, we retreat to our cottage in Pennsylvania. For this season, it's a rhythm that works. But make no mistake: It's one that's taken years of orchestration to put together.

Life impacts rhythms and rhythms impact life. Sit with that for a moment.

Rhythms look different if you have a newborn at home, if you're caring for an aging parent, if you're an empty nester, if you've just started a new job, or if you've just welcomed home a new puppy. We're still avoiding the puppy, much to the chagrin of our girls!

Rhythms have looked different when Emily and I were both working outside of the home and balancing childcare duties. Rhythms look different when your kids are playing on sports teams and have other extracurricular activities, or when they are off from school for summer break. Time, resources, physical energy, emotional energy, etc., are all impacted by life. Obviously, routines are most successful when they complement and work in tandem with your current rhythms. Simply put: *Routines are there to serve you, not to control you.*

Life impacts rhythms and rhythms impact life.

When you and the people you share a home with are in sync with one another, life feels harmoniously balanced. When you're not . . . well . . . you can connect the dots. At our best, Emily and I are a team, and we've learned that when life feels out of sync, we have to communicate with each other. We have to get to the bottom of what's going on. We've found that these questions are helpful to reflect on, and we try to carve out time to discuss them (when the kids are not around!).

- What is our current stage of life? How does this feel different from the others?

- Who am I responsible for? What am I responsible for?

- When do I feel most alive? What brings me energy?

- What are my pressure points? What takes away energy?

- What is one thing in my life that is causing me stress?

- What is one thing that we could change today to make life a little easier?

It can be helpful to consider what's going on—personally, professionally, and as a family—and what might be coming up in those categories in the next few weeks or months. These questions can provide the opportunity to talk about events on the calendar and unearth how you're feeling about yourself, your relationship, your parenting, and other important topics.

Adjusting What You Can Control— and Rolling with the Rest

If you are raising a toddler, you know how exhausting it can be. Mabel used to have a daily repertoire of ways to wake me up.

Emily was often up multiple times in the night with our second baby, so my routine was to be the one to get up in the morning with Mabel, very early. I had encouraged her to stay in bed until the sun was up, so she'd either scream *"Daddy, the sun is awake, the cows are mooing, the birds are chirping"* from her crib or climb out of it, toddle into our bedroom, and literally pry open my eyelids with her little fingers and say, *"Daddy, I'm hungry. Hungry, Daddy!"* Or she'd just hit me with a stuffed animal and say, *"Daddy, up!"*

The girl always woke up hungry, and I lived to serve. I'd slowly roll myself out of bed, turn on the living room lights, groggily walk to the kitchen, and cook Mabel a hot breakfast of her choosing. I see now (hindsight really is 20/20) that I may have incentivized this early wake-up, because I acquiesced in making her anything she could dream up: cinnamon rolls, scones, egg bakes, yogurt parfaits, you name it!

Then one morning I woke up much later than usual—and on my own. The bedroom was still pitch black, but I heard the faint sounds of someone moving about the kitchen—drawers being pulled open, the refrigerator being slammed shut. Then I heard the sound of eggs cracking. Something clicked for me. I pulled off the covers, ran to the kitchen, and found three-year-old Mabel standing on her step stool at the kitchen counter.

"I'm making eggies. Could you turn on the stove? I don't know how," she said.

I'd never been more grateful for our childproof stove knob covers.

From that moment on, I resolved to always wake up before her. I would beat her at her own game.

It initially took a few months to shift my sleep patterns and adjust my internal wake-up clock. I started by going to bed five minutes earlier and waking up five minutes earlier. I was gradually able to shift my sleep enough to wake up at 4:30 naturally. But to make this work, I have to go to bed early. I don't get less sleep than I did before, but I have shifted to have more awake time in the early mornings instead of late evenings. I've got to brag: I've been getting up since the butt crack of dawn for over five years now, and it's a rhythm that has transformed my life. Seriously.

Sometimes I enjoy thirty minutes or even an hour alone before one of the girls wakes up. Sometimes I brew some coffee and sit on the couch, enjoying the early morning silence. Or I read, write, journal, or pray. I also use part of the time when no one else is awake to clean certain areas of our apartment. Early morning, before the chaos starts, can be the most peaceful time of day to do something solitary that brings you joy.

I've realized that if I don't give myself the gift of quiet time in the early morning, it'll never happen. So much of our days can feel noisy and out of our control. I've come to really appreciate my morning quiet time.

Sure—I get tired. Sometimes mentally, sometimes emotionally, sometimes physically. Sometimes all three at once! I've learned that I can deal with physical exhaustion (or I can make an

> **Pro Tip**
>
> Tidying is the process of bringing order to things, and that includes your daily rhythms. So, ask yourself: "What is within my control to change about my daily rhythm and what is not?" Remember that rhythms change with the seasons of your life—no one routine will last forever! (Someday I'll be able to go to bed later and get up later, too.)

iced coffee), but it's tougher for me to handle the mental exhaustion. I'd rather get up tired than push "Snooze" and feel rushed and a bit frazzled all morning. Emily is *very* different from me in that respect.

I'm not trying to spark a debate about the virtues of being an early bird versus a night owl. I also recognize that the demands placed on fathers in the middle of the night during early parenthood can be very different from the demands placed on mothers. But I've found power in embracing the rhythms of life instead of fighting against them. There's value in making an overwhelming aspect of life feel more manageable. I've learned to name what rhythms are important to me, share those with the people I live with, and find ways to tidy them up. Sleep is so important, but quiet solitude is, too. Embracing early mornings has made all the difference *for me,* and finding your own solitude time may do the same for you.

Experimenting with Your Routine

My early morning wake-ups have been going strong for years now. I often share my routine in Instagram stories, opening with a greeting of "The sun is not awake, my children are asleep" because I am celebrating that I have taken back my early mornings. "Oh, good for you," you might be saying with an eye roll. But that routine started as an experiment. New routines don't always work out, but you have to try—and try again—to find ones that work for you.

Harness the Power of Yes; Embrace the Power of No

It's important to think about what you want your family's rhythm to look like, and then make decisions that support that. For our family, at this point, that has meant no extra-curricular activities during the school year. We like having two hours in the evening to move through the bedtime shuffle as a family. We like having our weekends open. Last summer our girls did swim team, gymnastics, dance camp, and archery, and having those extracurricular activities over the summer instead of the school year worked well for us. That doesn't mean that is the right decision for every family, but it's important to consider that a "no" to something can open space for a "yes" to something else.

I've found it helpful to try out new routines using a method that my friend Patty Morrissey refers to as the "Thirty-Day Experiment." This is what it sounds like: You identify a new routine that you think could enhance or support your life, and you fully commit to trying out that new routine for thirty days. During that time, you reflect, stay curious, and consider what you're learning about yourself along the way. Then, after the thirty days, you decide whether you want to continue with the practice or not. Either decision is okay. What's important is trying, then reflecting and learning.

I've experimented with personal routines, like no screen time on weekday evenings, reading a book on my lunch break, doing yoga in the mornings, or running home from work twice a week. Starting something new can be difficult. We encourage kids to do this all the time, but as adults, we sometimes forget how valuable it can be for us, too. Once you've started something new, there can be a feeling of internal pressure that you have to keep it going, forever. But it's time to let go of that pressure. Some of these experiments I've maintained, and others I've let go of, like no screen time on weekdays. I can't help it; I love to put on headphones and watch a show while I wash dishes. Especially the *Real Housewives*.

Different seasons of life place different demands on you, and experimenting with your routine can invite you to fully lean into the current rhythms of your life and consider a small way to solve a problem or tidy something up. Did I benefit from quiet mornings when I could choose how to spend my time before my kids woke up and I left for work? Yes. Does this mean that I'll be waking up early forever? No.

Revamping Your Routines to Match Your Rhythms

It's one thing to create personal routines for yourself, and another to create routines for others and expect them to happily and compliantly follow your directions. As a teacher, it's my job to build relationships with each student so that I can motivate and inspire them and meet their individual learning needs. It's like trying to solve a great psychological puzzle. Sometimes I feel like I have three psychological puzzle fronts: work, home, and my mind. Sound familiar? As adults, we're responsible for making things work, in spite of obstacles, and creating routines is often the best line of offense.

The purpose of routines is to solve problems and help free up desperately needed mental space by making habits and behaviors feel automatic. They tidy up a series of events that happen day after day. Routines are like anchors, and they can help provide structure, making things feel predictable. Holidays and summertime are exciting, yet can feel in sharp contrast to the rest of the school year because of the lack of predictable routines. There's a reason the lyric "And Mom and Dad can hardly wait for school to start again," from "It's Beginning to Look a Lot Like Christmas," is such a beloved refrain. For some, the lack of predictable routine can be unenjoyable and transitioning back to more structured time is preferable. Those transitions back take time, too.

If you have school-age kids, you know this to be true: August is as much a "New Year, New You" moment as January. Over time, I've learned that it takes our family about six weeks to get into the new routines again, and for things to feel predictable and, dare I say, joyfully mundane again.

When I was Dean of Academics, one of the responsibilities that I enjoyed most was coaching teachers on routines. I used a tool called a "Routines Framework" to help teachers break down the process for how to plan, experiment with, and reflect on a classroom routine. It's one thing to say, "All right, everyone, grab your math notebook and meet me on the rug," and another thing for thirty students to be motivated to actually follow all the steps that you expect them to.

Routines need a framework. Planning routines is a cyclical process, and walking through the framework with one routine—be it personal, household, or workplace-related—can be transformative. Once you envision one routine, you can apply aspects of that framework to others. Over time, and with a good amount of patience and practice, you can build your routine muscles. This is what it looks like:

Routine Framework

Plan the Routine
• What's the problem?
• What do you want to happen?

Experiment
• Try out the routine.
• See how it goes.

Reflect
• What's working?
• What's not working?
• How can you tweak the routine?

Move on!

Some routines feel daunting to tackle because there are *so many* steps involved. You can't just say to your three-year-old, "Get ready for school." There are so many interconnected and related steps that make that routine possible. A framework helps you to envision, break down the steps, and create an organized plan for moving forward. If you're not clear on the routine, how can you expect your kids or employees to be clear on the routine?

I know there are times when you've wanted to wave a magic wand to get all the laundry folded. Or to wave a magic wand to get all the kids in bed. Or to wave a magic wand to get the pile of papers on your kitchen counters to just *go away*! But I have yet to find the magic wand. The Routines Framework is as close as we've come! It invites you to slow down, to analyze, to assess the situation, and to approach what's happening in your home.

Troubleshooting "the Great Bedtime Shuffle"

"Having trouble getting kids to bed? Do they fight you when they know it's about that time? Remember to give enough notice to them so that they know it's coming up. I like to start right when they finish lunch."

That's a great line from Alyce Chan, a wonderful comedian who posted this quip on social media. It's funny and so *relatable.*

I like to call this "the Great Bedtime Shuffle" because it's that tricky period of moving kids between dinner and bedtime when logistically so much is happening—picture spaghetti on the walls and floor, dishes in the sink, homework spilling out of backpacks on the floor, plus little naked butts running out of the bathroom and through the kitchen. So much can go wrong!

A few months into the last school year, we decided to tackle this pain point. One evening, I was standing at the kitchen sink washing dishes while Emily was helping the girls in the bathtub. In the midst of their screams and squeals, one of the girls asked "Do we have time to play a game tonight?" and Emily said "Sure!" while I simultaneously yelled "No, we're out of time!" It dawned on us that we didn't have clear time stamps for how to manage the full two-hour transition to bedtime. My primary routine strategy was announcing, "It's seven P.M.! Everyone should be in bed!" Emily and I needed to align on how we wanted bedtime to play out, then share that vision with the girls and work as a team toward our collective goal. It currently felt like we were all fighting against one another.

So what did this revamped routine look like? Here's what we came up with:

> **Pro Tip**
>
> When introducing new routines to children, it can take at least six weeks for it to begin to feel predictable. Consider how you can introduce aspects of the routine over a six-week stretch of time. While we can sometimes feel motivated to "take on the world" and revamp *everything*, that mentality can quickly cause you to lose steam. Small, intentional steps forward often lead to the longest-lasting change.

The Great Bedtime Shuffle

5:00–5:30 P.M.: Dinner

- Eat dinner together
- Clear the table
- Begin washing dishes (Emily and Tyler trade off)

5:30–6:00 P.M.: Bath time

- Person not washing dishes supervises
- Matilda and Margaret—shared bath (both girls still need help)
- Mabel—individual bath (can bathe independently)

6:00–6:30 P.M.: Brush teeth, put on pajamas, prep for bedtime

- Person who was washing dishes supervises
- Matilda and Margaret—still need help with brushing teeth (they *do not* like minty toothpaste)
- Mabel—independent (check that she's used fluoride rinse)
- Make sure all girls are in pajamas
- Fill water bottles, place in beds

6:30–7:00 P.M.: Family choice / buffer time (provide choices)

- Family game
- Reading time
- Puzzle time
- Coloring
- Wrestling—the girls seem to want this every night!

In our current season, we're all out of the house the majority of the week. That's a major rhythm change for our family now that all three girls are in school and I think we've all felt the impact. Sometimes it feels like we're ships passing in the night. We're in this exhausting, messy, yet beautiful season of life, when we simultaneously crave more time with one another and also crave more alone time.

Being able to answer crucial questions—"What is the purpose of this routine?"; "What problem is it going to solve?"—is almost always the crux of the matter. We've learned that once you have a clear vision of what you want from a routine and have identified the current set of problems, you can begin to consider the series of steps that you could put in place with the goal of finding a solution to the problem. As you implement the steps, it's also important to remember to step back and consider when things aren't meeting your vision and tweak parts of the procedure. Reflective problem-solving is such an important part of designing and experimenting with new routines.

A DIY Routine Tutorial

Have you ever seen a piece of discarded furniture outside of someone else's home and think . . . *maybe?* I'm a "trash to treasure" artist, taking neglected dressers, bookshelves, and tables and turning them into colorful masterpieces. Experience has proven that what's tossed out can often become a canvas for transformation—paint works wonders. Routines, like paint, need time to settle between layers. Let's consider the parallels.

When painting furniture, the first step is sanding. Sanding removes imperfections and dimples, and ensures an even, smooth finish that will make the paint less likely to chip or peel. When creating a routine, you can always "sand" and reset things.

After sanding, you usually apply light, even coats of paint or stain. Allow time for each layer to dry, then apply as many coats as needed for full coverage. With routines, the same applies: If you try to add too many routines too quickly (without giving them time to "dry" or set first), you can create problems for yourself.

The final, most tedious step is to apply polyurethane to protect the furniture from future scrapes and spills. Polyurethane is notoriously difficult to apply, because if you apply it in really thick, splotchy coats, it's difficult to undo the damage without sanding or stripping the furniture all over again. That's why all the pros recommend applying light coats gently with a foam brush. Allow each coat to dry, and leave time (up to thirty days!) for the final coat to completely "cure" before starting to use the furniture.

When it comes to routines, take a cue from this layering process—don't rush it. Allow time for your efforts to "cure" and solidify. If you're considering starting a new routine, apply each part systematically, like layers, giving each one time to settle before adding the next. This approach ensures a strong foundation and lasting results.

Creating a Values Wheel

Musically my life symphony has a fast, up-tempo cadence, with the occasional cymbal drop for dramatic effect. Makes sense—I'm a father of three, a husband, a teacher, an adventurer, and also an aspiring stand-up comedian! Did you see that one coming?

A year before adding "comedian" to that list, I began negotiations at work to transition to a four-day teaching schedule. Since I was a kid, I'd dreamt of becoming a writer. I knew if I was going to turn that dream into a reality, I'd need to carve out more space in my life. See how I'm drawing a page from my own playbook?

One option was to do all my writing on nights and weekends, but I knew that would have a major impact on Emily and the girls. So, after nine months of negotiations with my school administration—yes, you read that correctly—I was able to arrange a schedule whereby I taught 80 percent of a normal workload for 80 percent of my pay and benefits. It was like the ultimate professional tidy-up project.

I had help negotiating this new schedule and navigating the transition to teaching four days a week from a former NYC school superintendent–turned life coach named Christina Froeb. I'd worked with her during my Dean of Academics days and now meet with her for coaching. To help me get my head around these changes she gave me an assignment that was transformative.

"I want you to think about your values in this current season. You have a *finite* amount of time in your day, and you can't give the same amount of energy to everything. I want you to think about eight core values, things that you hold sacred in your personal and professional life. Having a clear understanding of your values and the degree to which you are currently honoring them will help our work together," she explained.

What she said made so much sense. It can be difficult to make decisions for yourself without understanding your core values, your North Star, the things you hold to be true. Without a clear sense of your values, it's easy for your decisions and actions to be guided by the thoughts, feelings, and needs of others. For a long time, I'd tried that strategy. Shocker—it didn't work.

I took her assignment to heart. Here are the eight core values that I identified:

My Core Values

Family/balance: I want to spend time with my wife and children and feel like I have margin and space in my life.

Service to others: I enjoy being in a position to help others and find value in creatively thinking about how to solve problems.

Kindness: The world needs more empathy and compassion. I've realized that my vulnerability acts like a superpower and that with kindness I can help and inspire others.

Finances/provision: I want to provide well for my family, but I also want a clear definition of what is just enough. I've pursued more for the sake of having more, and I'm no longer interested in that.

Gaining influence: I want to write a book and share my "Tidy Dad" message. Notability helps books get into the hands of people, and I feel like I have a story to share.

Strategy: I want to make sure that my actions add value, and that I'm stewarding my time efficiently and productively.

Acknowledgment/legitimacy: Writing a book helps me feel like my message is legitimate and worthy of consumption.

Beauty: Aesthetics and organization are important to me. I thrive in calm environments.

On our next call, Christina invited me to place the values around a wheel and consider the degree to which my life currently reflected those values. I assigned each of the values a number from one to ten. The number one was the lowest level of honor, ten was the highest. Here's how my wheel took shape.

Creating my values wheel made me realize that even the most joyful, productive, exciting, and creative rhythms need to be in balance with the other aspects of life that we value. My hobbies and creative pursuits are great, but they can't come at a cost to my family and the time we have to spend together.

Values Wheel

1. Choose eight core values (see examples below) and place them around the wheel.
2. Use the scale 1 (lowest), 10 (highest) to assess how much you are honoring them.

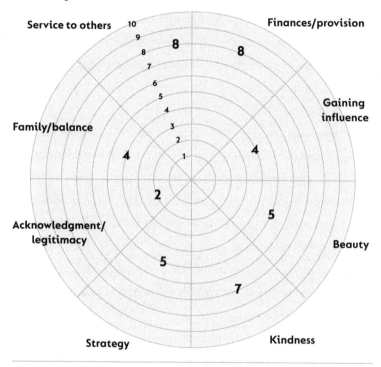

Start Small or Start Again

In many cultures around the world, people ring in the New Year with a Polar Bear Plunge. You've seen them on the news no doubt. Grown men and women strip down, run into a freezing-cold body of water, plunge, and then run out to put on a robe and drink some hot cocoa. Taking this to heart, on January 1, 2024, I put on my rubber ducky swim briefs and jumped into my sister-in-law's cold-plunge pool at her new home in Indiana. The cold water on my skin felt invigorating. I stayed in the water for nearly a minute and resolved to do a similar plunge in the lake at our cottage in Pennsylvania during the holiday break. I did it, too—even needing to crack the ice to make a place to jump in on the first day. I was feeling really great about starting my New Year with such gusto.

When I got back to New York, however, I had no place to plunge into cold water (the East River was both too far away and too gross, and I tried cold showers once, but it didn't have the same effect)—and my enthusiasm started to wane. It was dark and dreary, and the dismal nature of the season, plus transitioning my own children *and* my students back to school after an extended break, really got to me. One morning I hit "Snooze" on my alarm and overslept by a whole hour. Mabel had to shake me awake—she's still an early riser.

I say it all the time: "Routines are there to serve us, not control us." I knew it was okay to take a break from my routines, yet this particular January it felt nearly impossible to get back into them. I started to wallow and was really hard on myself. After all, I was Tidy Dad—it was my job to help and inspire others with their routines, and I couldn't even do my own. I'd started the year so strong. I mean, I'd broadcast to the world a video of me plunging into a cold pool in rubber ducky swim briefs, and now I couldn't even get out of bed. It felt like I was starting over again at zero.

Questions to Ask Yourself When Considering Your Rhythms and Routines

☑ Think about how you spend your day. What items in your day can you absolutely not function without? (Coffee, anyone?)

☑ Consider your current season of life. What are your needs? What are your wants? Is there anything getting in the way of those things right now?

☑ What are the pain points in your day? How could you streamline or eliminate them? Be creative!

☑ What's most important in your current season? Are you making space for it?

☑ What is your vision of a joyful life? What do you need to do to get there?

Why did it feel like I was starting at zero? Because I was! Transitions are difficult. So what did I do? I took my own advice and began to layer routines. The second week of January, I focused solely on waking up early again. That was doable. Then the third week of January, I focused on waking up early *and* cleaning one area of the apartment each weekday morning (which was really needed by then). Seeing the by-product of my efforts—a cleaner, tidier home—was motivating, and I started to gain back a little energy. Then the last week of January I started using my workout app and writing in my journal after I finished cleaning. I was adding my routines back on in layers and allowing time for them to dry.

Rut and routine are flip sides of the same coin. We've all hit those stagnant moments in life. But that January taught me something crucial: Everyone needs routines to smoothly move from one task to another, and establishing (or reestablishing) routines takes time. We understand this concept for kids, but adults need them, too! Just as a plan helps kids transition, adults benefit from a reentry plan after the holidays.

These transitions might feel like "surthrival" seasons—tough, yet revealing beauty. I've learned the power of taking small steps forward and reaching out for help.

INDEPENDENT PRACTICE

What's Working/What's Not

As you're probably learning, this book is less of a *do this, then that will happen* and more of one that focuses on the big-picture approach to managing and dealing with the messes you may experience. Because all of us are triggered by different messes in different ways. Apart from stepping on tiny toys. Our family loves playing with LEGO bricks, but when the pieces get left on the floor—*ouch!* That's a universal trigger.

When we're in a rut, it can feel like *everything* is going wrong. When things feel like they're starting to click, it can be difficult to step back and celebrate. But I invite you to practice the principle. I want you to grab your notebook or phone and make a list. Divide your paper into two columns and label one side "What's Working" and the other side "What's Not Working." Consider routines related to home, work, and your personal life. Get curious and ask yourself the following questions:

- How do I feel at the start and end of my day?

- What activities bring me joy or accomplishment in my current routine?

- Are there recurring obstacles hindering my productivity or well-being?

- Do my current routines align with my long-term goals and aspirations?

- Am I allocating *any* time for self-care or relaxation?

- What new routine would I like to experiment with for thirty days?

4

Embrace
"Surthrival"

For any number of reasons, there will be periods in your life when your rhythms and routines are upended and you'll have to work to keep your metaphorical head above water. At times like these, we need to intentionally adjust our mindsets to notice the small moments of joy within struggle or crushing monotony. This perspective shift can make all the difference and help you not just survive but thrive.

I've been teaching for more than fifteen years, yet memories from my first year of teaching at a rural school in Nicholasville, Kentucky, are still seared in my brain. Namely a student's dog pooping in the middle of my classroom during my first holiday party. Talk to most teachers, despite how many years they've taught, and they'll likely recount the experience of their first year in vivid detail. By the end of the school year I was exhausted and felt a bit defeated. I wasn't so sure this career path was right for me.

I wanted to go to graduate school—my idea was for an adventurous degree in comparative and international education—but Emily and I had decided to take turns. I would teach while she attended graduate school full-time, and then it would be my turn. It was difficult to wait. I knew we needed health insurance and a stable, albeit very small, income on which to live, so I knew I'd need to return to teaching in the fall.

Emily knew I was struggling, so we devised a way to give me what we hoped would be a battery-recharging adventure plus help me with my eventual graduate school application (which would be my ticket out of Kentucky and out of that school): I got a summer job teaching English in Bulgaria for two months! Sounds exotic and exciting, right?

Unfortunately, when I landed in Bulgaria, I discovered that the airline had temporarily misplaced my luggage, and I had to wait in the airport for twelve hours to get picked up by my group leaders. Not a great way to start my summer! And things didn't go much more smoothly once I'd been rescued from the airport and got situated in the home of my hosts, a Bulgarian widow and her elderly mother.

I'd been told that I'd have a full-time teaching placement, but it turned out that my schedule was reduced to only one hour per day. Although that may sound like a dream workload, instead of being rejuvenating, the resulting "free time" felt completely over-whelming. I was lonely, isolated, and could only communicate clearly with my English-speaking roommate, who had a different schedule.

Over lunch at the town orphanage (yes, you read that right—our program provided us with a small meal stipend, which could be redeemed at the local orphanage for only $1 per person), I realized that I had a choice to make. I could allow my loneliness and despair to completely envelop me or I could try to turn the isolation into a transformative experience.

I decided to make lemonade out of lemons and make it a summer of reading. I developed a routine of teaching in the morning and then walking through town and hiking to a small church in the hills above the town square. I'd sit and read for hours each day—I had packed a bunch of teaching books as well as *The Purpose Driven Life*—and lose myself in the reading and in music on my iPod. I had downloaded only a few songs (this was before Wi-Fi and smartphones), and to this day, whenever I hear Kelly Clarkson I'm instantly transported back to Bulgaria in my mind, sitting alone in a field next to a prayer chapel. I could appreciate that the place was beautiful, and I learned to tolerate if not enjoy the quiet and alone time.

"Surthrival"—the process of finding the growth potential during a time that might otherwise be stagnating or difficult.

Plus, the reading really did help my teaching that next year back in Kentucky! That's the year I would be named "Teacher of the Year" at my school and then for my entire district. Talk about a comeback story! This is a good example of what I call "surthrival"—the process of finding the growth potential during a time that might otherwise be stagnating or difficult.

Surthrival seasons often crop up around life transitions: graduating from college, planning a wedding, changing careers, having a baby, divorce, caring for aging parents, potty-training a toddler, moving. The common denominator is that a situation calls for a level of mental, emotional, and/or physical energy that outpaces your typical capacity.

I like to give my personal surthrival seasons titles like those of romantic comedies. Here are some of my favorites:

Crazy, Stupid Love Ends—my parents' divorce

50 Non-First Dates—our first years of marriage

Eat, Pray, Read—my summer in Bulgaria

The Out-of-Towners—moving to New York City

Sleepless in New York—teaching full-time and going to grad school

Cry-Baby—anticipating the arrival of our first daughter

Something's Gotta Give—negotiating four days of teaching

You get the gist—if I don't laugh, I'll cry. Surthrival seasons are like that. So how can you manage those seasons? Well, let's unpack a few strategies.

Break It Down to Manageable Steps

A retired teacher and seasoned veteran named Barbara Pollack acted as my fairy godmother during my first few years of teaching in New York City. I was balancing full-time teaching with graduate school classes at night, and my colleague Leah and I were tasked with building the instructional plan for fourth grade while also teaching two separate classes of fourth graders. As Barbara liked to say, we were "building the plane as we were flying it." Talk about surthrival.

To this day, I still use the instructional framework that Barbara introduced to us, and have also learned how to apply it to my life during seasons of surthrival. Mapping out an entire school year's curriculum is daunting work, but she taught us how to take complex goals—like teaching kids idea-generation strategies in fourth-grade writing—and break them down into increasingly granular, manageable, bite-sized steps. In the classroom, the process looked like this:

1. **Identify the scope and sequence.** This step encourages a teacher to articulate a helicopter-level view of the entire school year. What are the big goals? How much time do I have to devote to each one? In what order will I address each goal? You need to set your goals and put them into a logical sequence before you can break down the necessary steps to achieve them.

2. **Create a pacing calendar.** This exercise got us teachers to map out a kind of itinerary, a sequencing of the goals we

had articulated in Step 1, and assign specific goals to blocks of time. How will I allocate tasks across my timeline? Are there important days or times of year that I need to plan around? This calendar ensured, as Barbara used to say, that "the train keeps moving."

3. **Drill down to the unit plan.** In a classroom, "units" are like modules of teaching content. An effective unit plan considers the learning goals, how many and what kind of assessments will measure a student's mastery of it (tests, quizzes, presentations), and how instructional time will be allocated within the unit. What are the smaller tasks that make up each large-task category of work? How am I going to know when the work is finished?

4. **Create the lesson plan.** Now we're down to the nitty-gritty details—what's the day-by-day plan for each day within the unit? If the previous three steps to this planning process were done well, the only thing left to ask yourself here is the specific *what* of each daily lesson. This is when all the planning and preparing enables you to successfully complete the tasks.

This kind of intentional planning may look overly detailed, but teaching is a full-on block-and-tackle surthrival occupation. After all, if you don't give the kids something to do, they'll most certainly give *you* something to do. My point is that whether you're instructionally planning or trying to navigate a complex life predicament, being able to take the task and break it up into manageable, bite-sized parts can make it feel less daunting. How did I make writing this book happen? I mapped out a plan à la Barbara Pollack.

My mom experienced a major surthrival season when she was trying to transition her parents into an assisted living facility. My grandpa's health was rapidly deteriorating and his neighbors had started to notice peculiarities that indicated sharp cognitive declines. It was no longer safe for him to live at home, and my grandma knew he needed more care, quickly. She tasked my mom with making the financial and logistical transition happen, but complicating matters was the fact that my mom couldn't let my grandpa know that the transition was unfolding.

My grandparents were both born in the Depression era and had lived for decades with a hypothetical someday mindset. They were frugal and had saved everything, which meant that on the decluttering level alone my mom had her work cut out for her!

When she came across several old, nonfunctioning appliances, her mother said, "But I need to keep that knob just in case another similar appliance breaks."

While my mom was trying to get my grandpa to edit his fishing gear, he said, "I know I haven't been fishing in over thirty years, but what if someone invites me to go? I need to be ready."

When she stumbled on an expansive cache of pantry and toiletry items, and multiple rolls of wrapping paper from the 1950s? "I forgot I had it. But I'll use it sometime!"

Of course, through it all my mom wanted to respect her parents' desire to remain as independent as possible, yet it was also urgent they deal with these items, and the house needed to be sold. Taking on this in-charge role changed their dynamic—she was now the adult child helping to care for people who had once cared for her—and she worried she'd disappoint or emotionally set them off at every turn. Those decluttering conversations were often moments of levity, but overall my mom was both mentally and emotionally exhausted—confronting your parents' mortality is a doozy of a surthrival challenge.

My mom worked in a hospital laboratory, which, much like a classroom, runs efficiently because of a series of procedures. She embraced a similar system as a way to get her head around the very big task of preparing to move my grandparents out of her childhood home. She *really* embraced it, with stacks of index cards to prove it! From the snapshot of her plan on the following pages, you can see that it tracks to the classroom plan Barbara gave to me as well—taking an overwhelming project and breaking it into bite-sized, more manageable, if still exhausting, parts.

Big transitions like this are often marked with an intense level of work, surges of incredibly emotional problem-solving, and a looming deadline. Your first impulse might be to immediately start working, but if you can take the time to step back and assess the situation, get your thoughts organized, and consider how to create a sequential path forward, you can approach the season with a more positive mentality and even look for opportunities to thrive. Again, this process sounds a little bit like decluttering your physical space!

"Moving my mom and dad into the assisted living facility was really tough," my mom said. "But as my dad was rapidly

Transition Planning

Goal Setting

1. What's the goal? *Move parents out of their home—located in a remote area on a state road—to an assisted living facility closer to family and to their doctors*

2. How much time do I have? *Six months*

3. What are the big categories of things that need to be done?
   - *Choose assisted living facility*
   - *Prepare house for sale*
   - *Move parents to assisted living facility*

Time Allocation

1. What is the logical order in which large-category tasks need to be completed?
   - *Align with siblings on care plan for parents*
   - *Tour assisted living facilities*
   - *Choose assisted living facility*
   - *Secure specialized care for parents*
   - *Manage finances, health care, insurance*
   - *Implement decluttering plan*
   - *Prepare house for sale*
   - *Move parents to assisted living facility*
   - *Sell house*

2. How will I allocate tasks across periods of time?

   February: *Align with siblings on care plan for parents; tour assisted living facilities*

   March: *Choose assisted living facility; secure specialized care for parents*

   April: *Manage finances, health care, insurance; implement decluttering plan*

May: *Continue to manage finances, health care, insurance; maintain decluttering plan*

June: *Continue decluttering plan; prepare house for sale*

July: *Move parents to assisted living facility; sell house*

3. Are there important days or times of year that I need to plan around? Special circumstances to consider?

   • *Thirty-day waiting period for most assisted living facilities*

   • *Financial plan—lots of $ in bonds, need to cash every fifteen days to move money to liquid savings*

Work Plan

1. What are the smaller tasks that make up each large-task category of work?

   Each month should have its own individual plan, but let's zoom in to focus on the month of April.

Manage finances, health care, insurance	Implement decluttering plan
• *Locate US Savings Bonds (all carefully recorded in a green notebook) and take to safety-deposit box at bank*	*Work through decluttering items room by room in the house. Organize items into the following categories:* • *Keep* • *Sell* • *Donate* • *Discard*
• *Convert US Savings Bonds into liquid savings*	*Identify items and tasks that can be dealt with after move to the assisted living facility and prior to the sale of the house:* • *Large furniture* • *Yard maintenance*

Manage finances, health care, insurance	Implement decluttering plan
• Create life fact sheets—date of birth, social security numbers, military history, medical history, current doctors, medications, allergies	Organize and pack the "keep" items that will be moved with them
• Insurance plan—what role will the insurance company play in assisting with the cost?	Drop off the "sell" and "donate" items
• AVOID discussing sale of house with Grandpa	Dispose of the "discard" items

2. Whom can I enlist to help with this work?

    • *Brother and sister to collect parents' information for life fact sheets*

    • *Grandma is of sound body and mind to help; just be mindful of emotional state*

    • *Husband can help with diversion of Grandpa and can help with lifting, moving, selling*

3. How am I going to know when the work is finished?

    • *When I feel like I'm able to independently manage their finances, health care, and insurance*

    • *The house is ready to sell and the clutter will not dissuade someone from purchasing the house*

I can realistically go over to their house several days a week to actively declutter. Unfortunately, financial work has to be completed at the bank. Other management tasks can be done at home.

deteriorating, I'll never forget him saying, 'Janice, thank you for taking care of me and your mom.' He knew how much I love him, and I feel like I helped him get to a beautiful place of peace." To me, that was a sure sign that she'd surthrived.

Surthrival Season Strategies

Not all surthrival seasons require complex planning and strategic thinking. Sometimes you just need to change your mindset, try to embrace the unknown, or add a spice of joy to your life. Here are a few Tidy Dad–tested and approved surthrival strategies!

Embrace Joy Plotting

Like a lot of teachers (as well as many nonteaching, Monday-to-Friday workers!), I used to get a bad case of the "Sunday Blues" at the end of every weekend. Like clockwork, on Sunday afternoons I would begin to think about the upcoming week, anticipating the challenges and the meetings and the stress, and also dreading the ways I might fall short of what everyone needed from me. I can see now this was the ultimate case of "the glass is half empty" syndrome, because there were always a few things that I could anticipate going *right* for me every week; I just wasn't focusing on them. Now I do. I call the practice "joy plotting," and I make time for it on Sundays.

I take a few minutes to envision the moments of joy that I'm likely to experience in the coming week. I try to name at least *one* thing that I'm looking forward to each day. I've learned there is beauty in identifying joy even in the midst of the mundane.

Not all days, weeks, or months will be full of anticipated extraordinary moments, but if you make yourself name just a few things you're looking forward to—however small—I think you'll discover that you *can* expect moments of joy to come. Joy plotting every week does something to your psyche—I like to think you start to build up your "capacity for joy" muscles.

Reduce Decision Fatigue

In chapter 3, I described our weekly family tradition of Foodie Fridays—letting our girls choose a snack treat on the way home to end the school week. So fun! We've also recently instituted Friday pizza movie night. Sometimes I make homemade pizza, and sometimes we eat at our favorite pizza shop a few blocks from our apartment. Then we let the girls watch a movie until bedtime. Sometimes Emily and I watch the movie with the girls, and sometimes we watch something else in another room.

Do you know what doesn't happen on Friday nights in our home? Meaningful conversation! We're all too exhausted for that. We tried Friday family game night. We're too exhausted for that, too. We tried Friday family craft time. We were too tired to clean up the mess.

Recognizing the power of pizza and screen time on Friday nights was transformational and a smart parenting move for us during this surthrival season known as raising three little people. Acknowledging that Emily and I don't always *have to* watch the movie with the girls has been a smart move, too. Simply knowing that we always eat pizza on Friday nights means one less decision any of us have to make. That's liberating in and of itself.

During seasons of surthrival, name what is important to you and make space for that. Then declutter the rest. Remember that decluttering is mental and physical exercise, and the process of decluttering helps to reduce the number of decisions that you have to make, because there are fewer variables to navigate!

"Yay, Blah, Oops": A Dinnertime Conversation Strategy!

At the end of a long day it's often easiest to quickly characterize it as "good," "bad," or "fine" rather than to elaborate on the details of how it really was. But in our household, we've tried to stop defining our days so simplistically. Each day is made up of a series of interconnected moments that can cause us to experience so many different emotions or feelings. It can be helpful to let others in on the range of them.

A few years ago, we introduced the dinnertime practice of taking turns sharing "yay, blah, and oops" moments from our day. We go around the table and each of us has a chance to share a moment from the day that fits into each category, though no one is obligated to cover all three. Simply knowing that you'll get a chance to share the highs and lows of your day helps all of us open up. We don't have to bottle things up and pretend that every day was full of only "yays!" This process of classifying and sharing a variety of moments is a simple yet powerful way to reflect on a day and begin to process it together.

Carve Out a Little Time for Yourself

I give my students a weekly period of "choice time." Essentially, this amounts to: If they have worked efficiently during the week and finished their work, they get some time to do what they like. If they haven't, then they sit at the back table and finish up their work. The simple tenet is incredibly motivational—they work hard to make sure they can have that "me time."

Of course, there's a flip side to this: "Those who choose to have choice time at the wrong time don't get to enjoy choice time later." That's motivational, too!

This strategy works beyond the classroom. For instance, I grant myself choice time on the weekends, which means giving myself a little time for reading for pleasure, going for a run with Margaret in the running stroller, going for a swim, or watching a TV show of my choice. It's a short period of time when I'm able to choose what I want to do and not feel obliged to run my choice by *anyone else.*

Our opportunities for choice time are *somewhat* limited these days, but Emily and I try to trade off with each other during afternoons and weekends when we're with the girls to provide some space for one another to be "off" the parenting clock. Choice time has looked different for us in different seasons, but having choice over how you spend your time, even if it's a tiny—say, five-minute—pocket of time, can be so life-giving. Taking a quick walk or listening to music can be rejuvenating. Choice time can feel like oxygen when you're struggling to catch your breath.

We also make space for "family choice time," which means

taking turns choosing something fun for our family to spend time doing together. It doesn't have to be as epic as the movie *Yes Day*, but it can be an opportunity to do an enjoyable activity together or to try something new. It's also an invitation to intentionally give some undivided attention to your kids.

Embrace Scruffy Hospitality

We have a sign on the wall in our apartment playroom: "Life is a beautiful mess." This is something we absolutely embrace, and it's in keeping with a trend in entertaining that's called "scruffy hospitality." The goal of scruffy hospitality isn't to perfectly decorate your living space, or to create beautiful spreads of food, or to dress to impress.

Scruffy hospitality means letting the people you care about enough to invite into your home see you in a real and authentic way. It means allowing them to get a glimpse of how you *really* live. There's no better time for adopting this style than during times of surthrival. This is a time when you need to surround yourself with people who embrace you for who you really are and not judge you for who you aren't. Emily and I are fully on board! We say it's okay if dishes are in the sink, if the playroom isn't perfectly tidy, or if there's a bit of laundry that needs to be folded. Just make sure your toilet is clean, and let people come over!

Surthrival seasons vary for each of us, but there's strength in recognizing we can't do it all or be everything to everyone. Like the airplane safety instructions, we must put on our own oxygen mask before assisting others. This principle extends beyond planes—it's crucial to stop shouldering all the burdens. I've had to learn, firsthand, how to stop doing all the work.

INDEPENDENT PRACTICE

Two Sides of the Same Coin

I invite you to find a quiet and comfortable space where you can reflect without distractions. Grab a pen and paper or open your Notes app. Take a few deep breaths and clear your mind.

Then, reflect on a challenging period in your life when you felt like you were merely surviving. What situation were you facing? How did you feel during that time? What did survival feel like? What lessons did you learn?

Now shift your focus to a time when you were not just surviving but thriving. Think about a time when you felt challenged yet fulfilled and accomplished. What was the situation you were facing? How did you feel during that time? What did thriving feel like? What lessons did you learn?

Look at the reflections that you've written for both surviving and thriving and notice any common themes, strengths, or strategies that emerged. Consider how the lessons learned could inform your future approach to things. Sometimes surviving and thriving are two sides of the same coin.

5

Stop Doing All the Work

Work is work, but my goodness, society tells us otherwise. In different seasons of life, work inside of the home and outside of the home look different. It's important to lean into the rhythms of your life and consider how you can share, outsource, or eliminate overwhelming responsibilities.

A few months after my childhood bus driver asked me about the "For Sale" sign located outside of my family's home, our house was sold. I packed my things, and then unpacked them, in two separate homes: Mom's house and Dad's house. Seemingly overnight, my sisters and I went from a two-parent household, where my parents shared the responsibilities for cooking, cleaning, and caring for us, to living in two separate homes, where each of my parents independently took on the mental and physical load of caring for children, home, and career.

One thing that remained the same was that when we woke up on Saturday mornings, regardless of which house we were staying at, we had a list of chores. In the summertime we had to help with yard work and mowing the grass at two different houses. Maybe that's why it was my dream to move to NYC? Central Park is our backyard, and I'm not responsible for any yard work there! Looking back on that two-home season of my life, I have so much empathy for my parents, because at times the workload of a single parent must have felt insurmountable.

My perspective as a child of divorce has greatly impacted my views of work, both inside and outside of the home, as an adult. I'm writing this book through the lens of a married father of three, and have a capable, competent partner with whom to share the work of raising children and managing a home. I know that's not everyone's reality, and am also aware that titling a chapter "Stop Doing All the Work" could feel a bit triggering. But stick with me.

I fundamentally believe that work is work, whether that work happens inside or outside the home. Clocking into an office job is work. Caring for a baby and a toddler at home is work. Scrubbing the kitchen floor is work. Coordinating after-school pickup and drop-off is work. Caring for an elderly parent is work. Scheduling a doctor's appointment for your child is work. All of these things take time, energy, and varying levels of effort, but they are all work.

In order for you to stop doing all the work, it's important to have a clear understanding of the workload carried by *all* people living within the home. There's an age-old debate about whose responsibility it is to care for the home. Is it the person who spends the majority of his or her time there? Should tasks be divided based on gender? Or should things be more balanced? The answer is incredibly nuanced and, depending on whom you talk to, can stir up tense conversation.

When Emily and I were dating, "define the relationship" conversations were incredibly trendy. Now it's time to make "define the work" conversations trendy. Emily and I have had numerous discussions about what kind of chores we like and don't like, and have found a system to divide them up that works for our family. I prefer chores that allow me to move my body, have a clear start/finish, are consistent week to week, and don't require mental energy. For me, that includes chores like cleaning up after meals, doing laundry at the Laundromat, tidying up rooms at the end of the day, and deep-cleaning our apartment. During the workweek, my mental energy is focused on teaching, and I find chores that require additional mental energy draining.

> Household chores are work. Have you had a conversation with the people in your household about how to manage them?

Emily is more of an analytical thinker, and so she does most of our family's meal planning, grocery shopping, ordering online or shopping (clothes, shoes, toys, gifts, etc.), or anything having to do with phone calls or the computer, like scheduling appointments or paying bills. These types of chores play to her strengths. We work together or take turns doing the routine maintenance chores that neither one of us particularly enjoys, like helping the girls put away their toys, folding and putting away clothes, washing dishes, and going through the mail.

We've learned that tasks don't have to be divided "equally" to be divided "fairly." And we've learned that we have to talk frequently about this work! Since having our daughters, Emily and I have both juggled careers with caring for our kids and our home, and with *trying* to care for ourselves. There have been seasons when I've had to sprint home from work, literally—as in take my running clothes to school, change, and run home as quickly as I can—so that she could hand off caregiving roles to me and run to work herself.

There have been other seasons when we've had a nanny come to our house (my brother-in-law, if you recall) to watch the girls twice a week. And there were other times when I was home full-time on paternity leave and we shared caregiving responsibilities. We both actively parent our children, and in each season of life, the logistical coordination of work inside and outside of the home has taken careful planning and a healthy amount of compromise, trial and error, and shared decisions about what to let go.

When people talk about their workloads—the mental, emotional, and physical work that they take on both inside and outside of the home—it can be a powerful first step toward reducing some of the burdens that an individual person feels. You don't have to be married to have these conversations, but if you are, initiating this type of conversation could sound like: "How about tonight we spice things up and define our fantasy of how to divide household duties together?"

If you have roommates, talk to them. If you live with aging parents, talk to them. If you are co-parenting, talk to the co-parent! If you live alone with your cat, talk to the cat—"This litter box mess has got to stop!" As the girls have gotten older, we talk to them about work and have begun to transfer some of the work to them. Teamwork makes the dream work. Having a check-in conversation is a powerful exercise in stepping back before making an action plan to move forward.

Then get a follow-up conversation on the calendar! Schedule a time to revisit these questions, because maybe someone's mind will change on one or several of them. I have found that quarterly follow-ups are best—that's once a season if you live in a place where the weather and leaves change. Or once a financial quarter, if your brain works on that schedule. These conversations are important to have no matter who you live or work with—everyone has their own preferences and hot buttons about their home space and workspace and how the work gets accomplished. Talking about the issues is the key first step to reaching an agreement.

It's also important to have a shared system for remembering important dates, notes, to-do lists, and tasks. The mental load that you might be carrying is real, and different people's brains are wired differently. But there needs to be a shared language for handling the unseen work. We can't invite people to help, or to understand the work, if they don't know what we're balancing. Discussing these systems is an important part of the check-in process.

When you have an understanding of the work that you're juggling and make sense of the mess—in some ways, this process is similar to decluttering—you can carve a path forward.

I've found three approaches that can be applied to help you stop doing all the work: sharing responsibilities with those you live with, outsourcing responsibilities to others, or eliminating responsibilities, which means making certain types of work go away altogether!

Share Responsibilities

Mabel recently announced that when she grows up, she plans to be roommates with her friend Isla. Matilda, just two years younger, immediately chimed in that she would love to join them, but Mabel said that there "wouldn't be room." Choosing your own roommate is lovely, but as you likely know, sharing space with someone isn't always sunshine and roses. A woman I'll call Jamie recently shared with me a situation that demonstrates this point in dramatic fashion.

"Here's the issue," she began. "My roommate and I have lived in our apartment for a while now, and we recently had a couple take the third room. The new roommates were friends of ours, and we were excited for them to move in. Previously when we brought on a new roommate, we'd all sit down and have a conversation about the house, shared space preferences, and how we'd keep things clean. But this time we didn't do that."

"And . . . how are things going?" I asked.

"Well," Jamie said before a long pause. "We mentioned to them that we could rotate cleaning tasks by the week and drew up a little schedule that we posted in the kitchen. Since there are four of us now, we assumed that it would mean a lighter load for everyone. But they both work long hours, aren't home that often,

Define the Work

If you're inspired to have a "define the work" conversation, here are some prompts that might help to facilitate a fruitful conversation about the mental, emotional, and physical work that happens both inside and outside of the home.

☑ What are your pet peeves? What irks you? What doesn't?

☑ Do you enjoy work right now? If not, what is making that difficult?

☑ When do you work best? When do you have the most energy?

☑ What are your best skills? What skills are lacking?

☑ How do you handle stress? How does stress manifest for you?

☑ What is "just enough" for you in this season?

☑ What types of housework or chores do you enjoy, or at least feel like you can tolerate? Which ones do you really not enjoy?

☑ How are we going to share responsibilities? What do you need from me? (The goal isn't always 50/50, but what works for us right now.)

and one of them just doesn't know how to clean a bathroom. My other roommate or I end up *recleaning* the bathroom after her week. Also, she'll wash dishes, but only if they are her own."

"And how does that make you feel?" (Therapy was rubbing off on me.)

Jamie paused. "Super resentful," she answered.

Ya think?

As Jamie's situation makes clear, it's easy for resentments to build up when philosophies aren't aligned around how all the work is going to get done in a shared home. Or when you feel like *you* are the only one doing the work and that your work is going unacknowledged. Or when it's expected that you complete all the household work based on gender roles. As a "girl dad," that makes my blood boil.

We all make messes, and we can all learn how to clean up messes.

"I work from home several days a week, and she works long hours outside of the home. I wonder if I expect too much from her. Like should I drop the issue and just keep cleaning the bathroom?" Jamie asked.

My response?

ABSOLUTELY NOT!

I advised Jamie to talk to her roommate, to "define the work" and uncover the story that was underneath the consistently messy bathroom. Jamie assumed the roommate didn't have the skills to properly clean the bathroom, but what if there was more to the story? There likely was.

I don't believe "tidy" is either something you are or something you aren't. As with most things, there's a spectrum and a lot of gray area between Camp Messy and Camp Tidy. We're often quick to label ourselves or others as "tidy" or "messy," but I've found there's always a story behind the mess. Uncovering that story is an important part of sharing responsibilities.

Some people—often men—like to use an "I'm just a messy person" excuse to get out of tidying. Why do you think so many men who are messy around the house have a spotless car? It's because we all take care of the things that we care about. If you can take care of your car, you can learn how to take care of your house. If you can have a tidy desk at work, you can have a tidy closet. It takes the same set of skills; they just have to be applied in different ways. Not knowing *how* to clean something is never a legitimate excuse for someone else in the home needing to carry an undue portion of the work responsibilities. You can learn.

We all make messes, and we can all learn how to clean up messes. We're going to tackle that issue in the next part of the book.

Talking about work is the first step. Actually drawing up a plan for getting the work done is the next step, like a good old-fashioned task list. Determine *who* is going to do *what* and *when* they are going to do it. If you live with children, also consider how to involve them in an age-appropriate way. Kids of all ages

Clutter and Mess Know No Gender

There is this widely pervasive and destructive stereotype that boys are inherently messy and that those boys grow into men who don't see mess or clutter.

I think this generalization and many others are destructive to relationships both inside and outside of our homes. When I was a child, did my parents expect my sisters to have tidy bedrooms, but then walk past mine and say, "Oh, it's okay if Tyler's room is messy, he's a *boy*"? No, and I'm grateful for that.

If you live with others who "don't see the mess" in the same way as you do, then instead of making a parody video about them or perpetuating gender stereotypes by allowing them to "get a pass" from feeling responsible for tidying up too, it's time to talk. There's been a breakdown somewhere, long before that mess was created.

We're all triggered by different things. We each have different tolerance levels for mess. But I believe that tolerance levels actually have nothing to do with gender.

are capable of helping complete household tasks, but of course, intentional coaching and modeling is needed.

A few years ago, I had a video about the "Tidy Dad Family" go viral, and my statement that we work together as a team to manage our home struck a major nerve with some people. Some

Separate the Tasks

When it comes to organizing, tidying, and cleaning, the order is important. You can't clean the bathroom if there are toiletry items all over the sink and floor. You can't put away toiletry items if there's no clear place to put them. So, start with decluttering (remember to clear, sort, assess, and plan!), follow that up with making sure your organizational structures are in place, then tidy the items into those designated places, and then you're ready to clean. Skip one of these steps, and the management of a home can become overwhelming.

thought it was incredible to see how my wife, daughters, and I worked together to tidy, fold laundry, and care for our home. There was another group of people who said involving our kids in household chores was "stripping them of their childhood." I disagree. Our children also have plenty of time to play. The messes that they create are evidence of that!

One household chore we share with our kids is laundry. Kids can learn to help with this routine, but first, they need to be taught how. Case in point, our friends Patrick and Teresa, who have three children and recently had a laundry fiasco with their oldest son.

"The baggies of dirty laundry were like steamed dumplings," Teresa said, catching me in the hallway at church. Like us, they don't have a washing machine in their apartment, so they wash their clothes at the Laundromat. Their youngest son's potty-accident clothes were in a ziplock bag next to the laundry hamper, and their oldest son was tasked with doing laundry.

They told him not to open the bags *before* putting the laundry in the washing machine. He took that direction a bit too literally, washing and drying the family's clothing without ever removing the dirty clothes from the bags. Thus, the steamed dumplings analogy. Needless to say, they just threw out those clothes. A great opportunity to declutter, and a reminder that teaching your kids important laundry life skills might save them (and you!) from future steamy surprises!

> **Pro Tip**
>
> Laundry is a great routine to introduce to kids, because it involves skills like sorting (by person), categorizing (by clothing type), matching (socks), and the fine motor skills of rolling, folding, or hanging items. Even young toddlers can participate in certain aspects of this routine at a developmentally age-appropriate level. Start simple!

One or two times a week, Emily or I haul our family's bag of laundry down our three flights of stairs, walk it across the street to the Laundromat, and load it into the washing machine. I love that *everything* is washed in about thirty minutes. We typically just wash everything together in a giant washer on the cold setting. After the laundry is washed and dried, we bring it all back to our apartment, dump it on a bed, and work on folding together. Over the years we've implemented an "I Do, We Do, You Do" approach to laundry and other routines.

When the girls were very young, laundry was still an "I Do" routine. They were often in the same room with us as we were folding clothing, so that they were introduced to the process and

Teaching Kids to Complete Routines Independently

I Do	We Do	You Do
Name the routine	Complete the routine together	Child completes the routine with reminders
Model the routine	Coach the child to do the routine	Child completes the routine independently

we would say to them "we're folding laundry" and model the steps of the routine as they played nearby. At first Emily and I would fold all the clothes, and then we would put away their clothes into their drawers. We eventually moved on to a "We Do" routine, where we showed the girls how to fold washcloths and match socks, and they would work on folding those items while we folded more complicated pieces. We would also give the girls their folded stacks of clothes and show them where/how to put them away in their drawers. We gradually coached them through folding other types of clothing, like shirts and leggings. Now we are in the "You Do" stage of the routine, where our older girls can complete the process of folding and putting away their clothes on their own, with reminders. It's a process, but we all wear clothes and can all help fold clothes. Teamwork makes the dream work.

If you are sharing responsibilities with an adult who claims to not understand how to complete a task, then introduce that person to the powerful medium of YouTube. Did I know how to take apart the pipes underneath our cottage sink to fix a leak? No. But do you know how I learned? By watching a YouTube tutorial.

After you've defined the work and divvied up responsibilities, post the task list where everyone can see it. If you're motivated by a checklist, I suggest getting one that has a toggle slider, allowing you to manually move the "X" to a "✓" when the task has been completed. Our girls use one for their morning checklists. It's been highly motivating for them (more on this in chapter 10), and it might work for your house, too!

Outsource Responsibilities

"Mom, your plants look really pretty," I said during a recent visit to her house in Kentucky. "I feel like I'm constantly moving mine from windowsill to windowsill, trying to figure out what lighting they prefer. And when they wilt, I assume that's when it's time to water them."

"Oh, Greg helps me," she said. "He tells me when to water, when to test the pH level of the soil, and when to give each plant a little food."

"Um, Mom, who's Greg?" I asked.

"My little plant app," she replied. "It's called Greg, and he's so helpful."

Outsourcing the responsibility of caring for her plants has brought my mom a considerable amount of joy. As it should.

Outsourcing responsibilities can be a wonderful strategy to help you stop doing all the work, so you can free up valuable mental and physical space to complete the types of work that you enjoy.

Our different personalities, experiences, and skill sets mean that various types of work may stress us out more than others. In some cases, spending money to solve a problem can help to relieve some of the burdens that you may feel. This could look like ordering groceries to be delivered directly to your door, paying for laundry service, hiring a babysitter for a few hours, ordering takeout food, flying in your parent to help with your kids for a weekend, or springing for a house cleaner to deeply clean your home once a month.

This doesn't have to mean an increase in your overall monthly budget, but it does mean getting intentional about how you spend your money. Rather than shopping for recreation and buying another shirt, toy, or home decor item, could you spend that same amount of money on *solving a problem*?

Sometimes deciding that you'd rather pay to get something done instead of spending precious time doing it yourself is the sanest course of action. For the first eighteen months that we rented out our cottage as a short-term rental property, Emily and I were the primary house cleaners. After each rental we'd drive to the cottage, completely clean the house, wash and redo the bedding, and get everything ready for the next set of guests. We learned a lot about how to manage a short-term rental, but it was *work*! We eventually decided to hire a local cleaner. Even though it reduced the amount of money that we earned per rental, it has been well worth it. Sometimes we even have the cleaner come to the cottage after we've been the ones who stayed, so that we can enjoy our time there without cleaning and redoing everything before we leave. You don't need my permission to do this, but I'm going to give it to you anyway. Go for it!

In order to spend money to solve a problem, you need to first step back and identify what's a nagging stressor, and then figure out what could actually help to relieve some aspect of that stress. This looks different for each of us! Take cooking, for example. Emily and I both enjoy cooking, but we can easily feel overwhelmed trying to decide what to make for dinner. I love creatively thinking about what to make for breakfast. I can throw together a quick lunch for school. But in the evenings, my mind is like mush. I can't put together a coherent thought.

A few years ago we decided to solve that problem, and at the recommendation of Emily's sister, signed up for a meal planning service. For a few dollars each month, we get dinner menus with customizable shopping lists emailed to us weekly, which takes all the planning and mental stress out of the equation. We can shop according to the prepared list, and then cook. This simple hack has saved us so much headache. Before Audrey and Braden moved, they used the same service, and we'd occasionally trade off cooking for each other by doubling the ingredients and preparing the meals. Those nights when dinner was brought up to us in our apartment were heavenly. The money we spent to make this arrangement work was so worth it!

Adding cooked chicken to a store-bought bagged salad; having breakfast options stored in the freezer for busy mornings; discovering the value of an air fryer and teaching your kids how to use it; arranging potluck-style meals with family and friends for holidays; hiring someone to mow your lawn; picking up a fresh cup of coffee on the way to work; ordering groceries so that you don't have to take your children to the store with you; purchasing a wet/dry vacuum or robot vacuum to help keep your floors clean. These are all examples of ways to outsource responsibilities. Outsourcing doesn't just mean hiring an employee, although I do have a friend who hired a temporary virtual assistant as a birthday present to herself, to manage personal work (e.g., scheduling, responding to email, performing various tasks). Outsourcing is a tangible strategy for reducing some of the work burdens that you may be facing, both inside and outside of the home.

Eliminate Responsibilities

Do you know the book *Alexander and the Terrible, Horrible, No Good, Very Bad Day*? Well, I recently had a day reminiscent of Alexander's when everything seemed to go wrong. In the morning before school, one of the girls clogged the toilet in our apartment bathroom, causing it to overflow and flood into the downstairs neighbor's bathroom. Over my lunch break the ranger called from our neighborhood in Pennsylvania to let me know that a tree had fallen on our cottage, splintering the soffit on the side of the house and damaging our roof. After school I took the girls to the dentist and one of them had a cavity in a hard-to-brush spot in her mouth. When the dentist told me, my eyes welled up with tears.

"I have some extra time right now," the dentist said. "Do you want me to go ahead and fill the cavity so you don't have to schedule another appointment?"

I told her that that was the nicest thing to happen to me all day.

We all have different thresholds in regard to the amount of work that we can realistically take on. That day I'd nearly reached my limit for mental and emotional work.

Earlier that morning I'd helped my downstairs neighbor clean up the bathroom and then texted the landlord, who promptly sent a plumber to fix our toilet. By the end of the day, I had also scheduled an appointment to get the tree removed from our cottage roof. I was in a heightened state of surthrival and was just trying to get things done. The dentist helped more than she could have known.

Last school year, my co-teacher Kierra and her husband finally purchased a house in New Jersey. For the remaining six months of the school year, due to traffic, she commuted over three hours round trip to school each day. She loved working with me— I mean, who wouldn't?—but the commute was crushing. So what did she do? She found a job at a school twenty minutes from her house and eliminated her killer commute.

My older sister, Amanda, lives alone in an apartment and has recently gotten several job promotions. People keep asking her when she's going to buy a house, but that would mean she would need to take on the full responsibilities of home ownership and home maintenance by herself. It doesn't mean she will never choose to purchase a home, but right now, her apartment is just enough for her. So what did she do? She signed her lease for another year, eliminating the need to take on more household work.

Eliminating responsibilities can be a wonderful way to stop doing all the work. If you don't like driving to work, then live somewhere close to your job or with public transportation access. If you're tired of caring for your large home and want to travel, then sell your house and move into an RV—that's what Emily's parents did. If you don't like dealing with your finances, then give away all your money.

I'm kidding with that last one.

At the core of my message is the power of creative problem-solving and choice. Each of us holds the power to decide how we allocate our time, energy, and resources; sometimes we just need help. By pinpointing the pain points in our work, we can devise strategies to manage them effectively. Asking for help is okay. Balancing work inside and outside of the home isn't a one-size-fits-all endeavor, but understanding our personal limits helps shape an action plan.

Unearth Your Personal Mess Threshold

News flash—we all have different thresholds for mess. In this exercise, I encourage you to explore your comfort level with different levels of clutter in various categories. By understanding your tolerance for disorder, you can make informed decisions about organizing your living or working spaces and communicate your preferences to others you share space with. Quickly assess, on a scale of 1 to 10, your mess tolerance in the following categories:

1. **Physical space:** Rate your comfort level with the cleanliness and organization of your physical space, such as your home or workspace.

2. **Personal hygiene:** Rate your tolerance for messiness in your personal hygiene habits, such as grooming and cleanliness.

3. **Work or study space:** Rate your preference for tidiness and organization in your work or study space.

4. **Digital environment:** Rate your comfort level with the organization of your digital files, emails, and online spaces.

5. **Social interactions:** Rate your tolerance for messy or complicated social situations, including conflicts or drama.

Take a moment to review your ratings and reflect on your personal mess threshold. Consider how your comfort level in each category may impact your daily life and decision-making processes. Then share these findings with the people you share space with!

PART TWO

TIDY UP
YOUR SPACE

6

The Order of Things

Organizing a cluttered space is challenging. Tidying an unorganized area is tough. Cleaning a messy space is daunting. It's time to connect the dots between these household systems, undertake them in a specific order, and establish consistent routines that feel manageable to you.

When I was featured in an "Instaparents" segment for *Good Morning America,* my grandma was super proud of me. She took her iPad with her to dinner that night in her assisted living facility to show her friends the online clip from the broadcast. She told them her grandson was a *celebrity.*

I'm not quite sure about that, but Emily and I were proud, too. I'd transitioned from school administration back to teaching and had started blogging as Tidy Dad. After a series of cleaning videos I'd posted on Instagram went "viral," I was invited to make my morning show debut. It was an honor to be given the opportunity to share my tidying journey with America.

The segment included an interview filmed in our apartment. The day before the segment was filmed, I took a personal day from work so that Emily and I could tidy the entire apartment. I wanted to ensure that every inch was artfully arranged to look *picture-perfect*. After a marathon tidying session, the apartment looked amazing, but our challenge was to keep it that way until the start of filming the next morning.

"You can't touch anything. *I mean anything,*" I said lovingly yet sternly to the girls when they got home from school.

> ## Our goal is not to live in a home that's "always tidy," but instead one that's "easily tidied."

In other words, what you see on television, in magazines, and online is not always the *full* story. The next morning, the film crew entered our immaculate apartment, set down their camera equipment on one of the shelves in the playroom, and the shelf fell off the wall. The crew was deeply apologetic, and we were able to film around the mess. As soon as the segment wrapped, life in our apartment returned to regularly scheduled programming. We served a meal, playtime happened, and the everyday messes of life returned. And you know what? That's okay.

After all, our goal has never been to live in a home that is always picture-perfect. If that was the goal, I'd have to teach my children how to levitate, give away all their toys, and only serve them foods that don't make crumbs. Fortunately, our goal is not to live in a home that's "always tidy," but instead one that's "easily tidied." That feels a lot more doable.

Sharing practical, routine-driven approaches for organizing, tidying, and cleaning is what I've become known for as Tidy Dad. That's what part two of this book is all about. To get started, we first need to quickly discuss those three distinct household activities and get clear on the differences between them. Organizing, tidying, and cleaning build upon one another, and I recommend tackling them in *that order.* Then we'll apply these routines to different rooms in the home.

I believe that consistent routines can make life feel a little easier and create more space for what matters. It's time to work smarter, not harder. Sometimes small changes can make a big difference. If your current routine isn't working, you can experiment with a new one.

I'm going to share some examples of what's been working in our space so that you can consider small changes or adjustments to your own space. I'm not going to outline a one-size-fits-all approach, because that's not realistic. Life looks different for each of us, and it's important to consider your personal season of life when creating routines and allow them to change as needed. I've said it before, routines are there to serve you, not control you.

Get Clear on Your Organizational Style

Simply put, organizing is the process of deciding where items go within your home and how those items will be contained within those areas. Everyone has their own particular organizational method to their madness. Want to know yours? Ask yourself:

Macro vs. Micro: Do you like organizing things into broad categories (like all the art supplies in one large bin) or do you prefer organizing items into more specific, smaller groupings (like markers in one bin, crayons in one bin, colored pencils in another bin)? How do you prefer to put things away, and which systems are the easiest for you to maintain and continue to use?

Visual vs. Nonvisual: Do you prefer to see the items you use regularly (on open shelving and in baskets) or do you prefer hidden storage (in cabinets and drawers)? Again, how do you prefer to put things away, and which systems are the easiest for you to maintain and continue to use?

Still not sure? Look at your bedroom—that's a place where most people's tendencies are revealed! How do you organizationally maintain the items that are yours? Understanding your habits, tendencies, and preferences (and those of your space-sharers) is key to helping you create effective organization systems that work for your home.

Of course, it's difficult to set up those systems without first decluttering the excess. My cousin Shannon's experience gives us a great example. She'd seen photos of my own tiny closet and was inspired to organize the closet in her new apartment. She loves fashion, skin care products, and a good handbag. Her goal was for her closet to look like a boutique store, with colorful displays, space between hangers, and a beautiful jewelry collection, but she couldn't make this aesthetic work in her smallish closet.

When I took a look at the issue, I realized that Shannon's bedroom closet had become a catchall storage area. (An "out of sight, out of mind" approach to closet storage clearly runs in the family.) I encouraged her to start by taking everything out of the closet and into the open and loading back in only those things that met her aesthetic goal. Once she'd artfully arranged her favorite clothing, shoes, bags, and jewelry in a fancy boutique style inside her closet, she and I could both see what was left . . . and where the problem had been hiding. It turns out that what had been getting in the way of her ideal closet ended up being old textbooks from college, purses from middle school, and clothing that she was ready to donate. Getting her to sort and assess all that had been in the closet was the key to establishing an organization to it that also lived up to the feeling she wanted the closet to give her.

If you share a home with kids, aligning organizational systems with their developmental needs and daily routines is empowering. The goal is to reduce or eliminate the "Hey, where is my . . . ?" type of questions by designing systems that solve pain points for kids and encourage them to own the organization of their spaces. As adults, we can become frustrated when we can't find the things we need, and it's the same for kids.

Organizational Systems for Kids

- **Clear Containers:** Clear containers allow kids to easily see what is stored inside. Small, stackable bins with attached flip-top lids can be incredibly helpful for organizing small toys. Large bins can be notorious clutter traps! When possible, replace large containers with several smaller ones.

- **Labeling:** Labeling containers can help kids easily identify what is stored inside and help prevent them from just rifling through or dumping items until they find what they're looking for. Young kids may benefit from picture labels before progressing to word labels.

- **Rainbow Categorization:** Sorting items by color can help reduce visual clutter and is an organizational system that even young kids can understand and also maintain. Clothing can be organized by category of item and then put into a closet or drawer by color. Rainbow categorization can also work well for organizing books on a shelf and add a beautiful pop of color to any space.

- **Alphabetical Order:** Thank goodness the "ABCs" song is so catchy. If you have a large assortment of items like books or board games, older kids may find they are visually easier to locate if they are organized alphabetically.

- **Low Hanging Hooks:** Hang it! Reach it! Use it! Don't underestimate the power of a low hanging hook. Kids can independently access the things they need when they are stored on their level. Hooks are a low-cost, high-impact way to make bath towels, coats, backpacks, headphones, and more accessible.

- **Go Vertical:** As your kids get older and grow taller, swap out lower storage pieces like a three-tier rolling cart for taller pieces like a bookshelf. Speaking of going vertical, if you're really tight on floor space, you could invest in one of those vertical Velcro space beds astronauts use. Your kid just might love it!

It's "Tidy Up Time"

I love the feeling when our entire apartment is tidy. When things are off the floor, off the furniture, and put away, I can more easily relax in our home.

Tidying is the practice of putting things back in their designated location. It helps ensure that when you need something, you know exactly where to find it, without having to ask another person. If you've first decluttered and organized the items in a specific space or room, tidying that space will be all that much easier!

I think it's important that from a young age kids learn how to care for their things. Caring for their things includes putting things away after they are used. Our apartment space begins to feel overwhelming when it seems like the playroom has started to empty itself into every other room. Life happens, messes happen, but our goal is to be able to easily reset the apartment back to factory settings. Tidying is a daily part of our family rhythm. It's predictable and it's mundane, but I've found ways to make it fun.

These strategies are a way to playfully experiment with tidying up play spaces:

Ten "Tidy Up Time" Strategies with Kids

1. **I do, we do, you do:** This is a strategy that we discussed in chapter 5 for laundry. "I do" is the process of modeling for your kid how you would like a task completed. "We do" is

the process of working together to complete the task. "You do" invites the kid to complete the task independently. This three-step strategy is a predictable instructional rhythm that happens every day in an elementary school classroom. Why? Because it's effective!

2. **Pick a color:** Designate a color for your kid to pick up. For example, "I want you to pick up all the blue blocks, and I'll pick up all the green blocks." This helps to make an overwhelming tidying task more specific and focused, and can also help to build color recognition skills in your young tidiers.

3. **Basket training:** Place a basket in each shared space. Use this basket as a catchall for objects that need to be put away during a tidying session. When it's time to tidy an area, invite your child to grab the basket and pick up any play items from the floor. When the basket is full, it's time to put things back in their designated organizational location.

4. **One minute per age:** You can't expect a toddler to have the stamina to tidy up an entire playroom for thirty minutes. Rather, we have found that a realistic expectation is around one minute per age. Even toddlers can often follow one- and two-step directions that help with the process of tidying, like "Let's work together to put all these blocks into this basket." This is a simple, straightforward task that can be completed together in two or three minutes, and still teaches kids to put their items away.

5. **Put on some tunes:** Turn "Tidy Up Time" into a dance party. Put on some fun music and dance while you put things away. You can even turn this party into a game of freeze dance. When the music stops, everyone stops tidying and freezes . . . and then starts again!

6. **Tidy the "secret" item:** If you have multiple kids tidying together, this is a fun strategy to try. Choose a "secret" item that needs tidying up in a room. Tell your kids you're going to watch to see who tidies up the "secret" item, but don't reveal the item until the space is reset. The one who tidied up the "secret" item wins, and you can decide the appropriate prize.

7. **Messy kid game:** It can be fun to place the blame for the creation of a play mess on another kid, especially an imaginary one. Our girls are huge fans of this game. I knock on the playroom door with a baby doll in my arms, and then ask them which of the other babies made a mess of the playroom. They tell me the story of how the mess unfolded as we work together to tidy things up. I ask questions that help to build the tension, and it's always fun to hear their answers!

8. **Beat the clock:** Set a timer and work to tidy in a race against the clock. Visual timers can be helpful for this, so that kids can see the countdown and know how much time they have left.

9. **"I bet you can't . . .":** Kids love an opportunity to prove adults wrong. Make a statement about tidying that you

"bet" your kid can't do. It sounds like, "I bet you can't pick up all those blocks with just one hand!" or "I bet you can't put your stuffed animals away while hopping on one foot!" You might be surprised to find that your kids are eager to try out a new method of tidying—and to win the "bet"!

10. **"For" vs. "with":** It's okay to occasionally drop expectations and just tidy things yourself. I like to turn on my favorite show, put on some headphones, and *fully* reset the play space when I tidy "for" our kids instead of "with" them.

Cleaning Like a Boss

Margaret had been in preschool for less than a week when I heard a familiar refrain from the playroom. "Clean up, clean up, everybody everywhere."

"Are you kidding me?" I said, turning to Emily. "How do we make it stop?"

If you were born or lived anytime around the '90s, you're likely familiar with Barney, the lovable (and slightly odd) purple dinosaur that uses a friendly, optimistic, and huggable attitude to convey educational messages. *"Clean up, clean up, everybody everywhere. Clean up, clean up, everybody do your share"* was his mantra.

I believe that song has single-handedly led to the mass confusion that adults of a certain age have toward the definition of "cleaning." The music video shows Barney and friends taking off their smocks after they've been painting and then hanging them on hooks in the back of the play area. Then Barney and friends take all the dishes that are sitting on the table and put them in the sink area. The friends work together to clear the space, but there's one set of tasks that is missing from the video: *the actual process of cleaning*!

What Barney got *right* was casting as a playroom friend a young Selena Gomez, who ultimately has gone on to become a wildly successful actress, singer, and mental health advocate. What Barney got *wrong* is that cleaning is not the same as tidying.

Let's be clear—cleaning is the process of removing dust, dirt, and germs from surfaces.

And let's be real—most people don't love to clean. The thing is, I do!

Before Emily and I had kids, I looked forward to my marathon cleaning routine on Saturday mornings. I would turn on a great podcast, and clean, clean, clean. After a long week, it was almost therapeutic. I'd work my way from the back of the apartment to the front while Emily simultaneously worked on household tasks that took mental energy, like planning meals or paying bills. In an hour or two, we would have a perfectly clean apartment that could be maintained until I cleaned again the next weekend.

Once we had kids, cleaning no longer took just a few hours. It seemed to take *all day*, because my three walking tornadoes were simultaneously making messes all around me. It's also not how our family wanted to spend our weekends—we wanted to make space for adventures!

I believe certain consistent routines can make life a little easier, and create more space for what matters. I experimented with cleaning a little bit of our home each day and eventually developed a weekday cleaning routine with a checklist. One week, I set up my tripod in the corner of the room I was cleaning each morning, and filmed a time-lapse video of the cleaning process. At the end of the week, I compiled the videos into a reel and posted it on Instagram. It became my first "viral" video.

Thousands of people have downloaded my weekday cleaning checklist; others asked if I'm bothered by the fact that this strategy means that all the rooms in our home are never completely clean at the same time. That's an easy question for me to answer: no. Because we have organizational systems in place, we can quickly and easily tidy up our home so that it appears orderly and "clean." Only Emily and I know that the actual cleaning is done on a rotational basis. Well, okay, now you know, too.

I typically set a timer for fifteen minutes in the mornings, and that gives me enough time to thoroughly clean one room/space. Obviously that's because my rooms are small; if you're going to scale up your square footage, you will also have to scale up your cleaning routine.

However, in a larger home, the entire space might not need to be part of your weekly cleaning routine. Make it work for you! In our small apartment, we use every inch of square footage every day. In a larger home, all areas might not be lived in equally. You might have rooms that you've never even been in! Take, for example, the woman who lives in a castle and asked me for a strategy to prevent her from losing her glasses. She also asked if I could advise her fellow castle owners in her online group about

Three Types of Cleaning

The foundation of the United States government is a belief in the separation of powers into three distinct branches: executive, legislative, and judicial. In cleaning, there are also three separate types, which each have a distinct and important role.

1. **Surface cleaning:** Removing visible dirt and grime. Think wiping down your kitchen counters after you've cooked or wiping toothpaste off your bathroom mirror.

2. **Deep-cleaning:** Using a bit of elbow grease and cleaning hard-to-reach places. Think cleaning underneath the refrigerator, moving the couch so that you can vacuum behind it, or pulling up rugs to clean floors.

3. **Sanitizing:** Using cleaning solutions to kill bacteria, fungi, viruses, and other pesky microorganisms. Think cleaning up after someone is sick, wiping down toys after a playdate, or getting your toilet bowl to shine like the top of the Chrysler Building.

how to more efficiently clean, because there were so many wings in their castles to maintain that it was beginning to feel like a full-time job.

I joked to her that I am but a common peasant and didn't know anything about cleaning castles, but the truth is that I do know it's helpful to take an overwhelming task and break it down into smaller parts to make it feel more manageable. That's what my weekday cleaning checklist is designed to do. For someone living with such an abundance of square footage, a cleaning checklist is going to be that much more helpful. I suggested she put herself on a schedule, tackling one room or space in her castle per day.

I kind of feel like a superhero when I'm cleaning, which is why last Halloween I dressed up as a superhero named Tidy Dad, cape, blue "Tidy Up Your Life" underoos, and all! Superman's main foe is Lex Luthor, and I guess you could say that my main foes are dirt, dust, germs, and grime. Superman has a cape. Batman has a Batmobile. Wonder Woman has her Golden Lasso. At this point, I really need a cleaning tool belt!

Here's what I'd keep organized on the belt:

Pro Tip

It's difficult to clean a space that isn't tidy, so in the evening our family tidies the space that I'm going to clean the next morning.

This way we're deeply tidying one location each day, which makes it much easier and faster to deeply clean that area the next day. This weekly flow helps to reduce the mental headache of remembering what was last cleaned when, and speeds up the entire process.

Tidy Dad's Top Ten Cleaning Tools

1. **Swedish dishcloth:** This is like a mix between a washcloth, a paper towel, and a sponge. It is very absorbent and can be used again and again to soak up spills, scrub out sinks, and wipe surfaces. You can rinse and hang it to dry between uses or sanitize it by microwaving it for thirty

seconds. To thoroughly clean it, put it in the washing machine and then lay it flat to dry.

2. **Microfiber rag**: This versatile rag helps to remove dust, dirt, grime, and fingerprints. It can also be thrown in the washing machine and used again and again.

3. **Brush set**: Helpful brushes for cleaning include: deep-cleaning brush, bottle-scrub brush, multi-angle brush, hand brush, and detail brush. If you have an old toothbrush, that can actually come in handy for cleaning grout and other small areas, but be careful not to mix it up with your actual toothbrush! The toilet brush is your best friend when it comes to cleaning one of the dirtiest parts of your bathroom. These are now available in a range of styles, including ones with advanced technology that self-sanitize after use.

4. **Sponge**: Similar to a brush, with an assortment of options: abrasive, Dobie, dry, cellulose, wire, microfiber, natural, Magic Eraser, etc. Try out a few styles, choose your favorites, and then keep them on hand to clean a variety of surfaces.

5. **Steel wool**: This acts as a coarse sponge that can be used to scrub different types of surfaces. It is available in several grades, which measure the coarseness of the steel, from super fine to extra coarse. Super fine steel wool can be used to scrub glass and windows, while extra coarse can be used to strip paint or remove rust, with a range in between. Pro

tip: If you live in an old house or apartment and have a mouse problem, try stuffing steel wool into holes or cracks under cabinets. That's where the mice usually get in, but they can't chew their way through steel wool!

6. **Polishing cloth:** After cleaning surfaces, you can use a polishing cloth to help bring faucets, mirrors, knobs, and the shower head back to brilliance.

7. **Spray bottle:** A glass or plastic spray bottle can be used for storing homemade cleaning concoctions or refillable pouches of cleaning solution, so that you aren't purchasing a new bottle each time. I also like to keep a separate spray bottle ready with only water inside for my littlest cleaning helper. Margaret loves to spray surfaces with water and then wipe them down with a rag. It's a simple strategy, but actually does help to keep things clean.

8. **Pressurized steam cleaner:** This cleaning tool makes me feel the most like a superhero! It harnesses the power of water with a pressurized steam clean. Steam cleaners typically come with a variety of attachments and are a chemical-free way to deep-clean. Ours is designed for cleaning hard surfaces and works well on grout, tile, and windowsills.

9. **Portable upholstery/fabric steam cleaner:** For cleaning softer surfaces (like couches, upholstered chairs, carpets, rugs, mattresses, and other types of fabric) you can use a portable steam cleaner. This provides a non-pressurized

steam clean for tough spots and stains and can help remove odors. It can also be handy for cleaning up after pets or used to clean car interiors.

10. **Plunger:** Does this really need a description? There are some pretty fancy plungers on the market now—larger ones for toilets *and* smaller ones for sink drains and tub drains! It's helpful to have both types on hand and to keep them easily accessible for your guests to spare them that awkward "Could you tell me where your plunger is?" moment.

INDEPENDENT PRACTICE

Where's the Breakdown?

Organizing, tidying, and cleaning are intricately linked; each relies on the others. When one system falters, it's crucial to pinpoint the breakdown and address it head-on. By reflecting on these questions, you can uncover areas for improvement and develop strategies to create a more harmonious and functional living environment. But remember, you're not going to do all the work. Here are some questions to ask yourself:

- Which specific area of my home feels the most chaotic right now, and what factors contribute to its disarray?

- How often do I consciously make an effort to return items to their designated places after using them? What obstacles or distractions hinder this habit?

- What motivates me to maintain a clean and organized living space, and are there times when I find myself caring less?

- Which areas of my home have been neglected and are in need of a little TLC to restore order and cleanliness?

7

Living Rooms and Dining Rooms and Playrooms, Oh My!

Your home's shared spaces are where life unfolds. Consider your family's rhythms and routines and how these parts of your home can best support them. Organize these spaces to flow seamlessly, adjusting as your life evolves.

Before we had kids, we used to host a lot of dinner parties in our apartment. There was always food, fun, and usually an apartment tour. Guests were often intrigued by some of our apartment's oddities. We have two entryway doors, closets in only one of the two bedrooms, and you can look directly into our bedroom window from the living room window. Three of our windows look directly into an open-air shaft that connects to the next building, so our neighbors' windows are less than three feet away. We've invested in some quality shades.

Architecturally we live in a "railroad"-style apartment, which is long and incredibly narrow, and all the rooms are connected.

This means we have to walk through one room to get to the next, and there is no separate hallway. The rooms *are* the hallways.

It's a strange layout, but it has its charms. There is a narrow bonus room that connects the kitchen and living room to the two bedrooms. It's a layout that can work well for families, as that bonus space can be used as an office or playroom, an area we've noticed is often lacking in many square-shaped, two-bedroom apartments in our neighborhood. The way we have used that bonus space has continued to change over the years.

No matter your square footage or the layout of your home, shared living spaces often evolve for all of us. Working from home might necessitate converting part of your living area into an office. A New Year's resolution to work out more often might lead you to plonk a stationary bike in front of the TV—bingo, now your living room is partly a home gym! A new baby or grandparents moving in might create a domino effect of still more changes.

When designing the shared spaces in your home, there is no more important guiding principle than paying attention to the rhythms and routines of *your* family. You need to assess the way you use your space and organize it for an ideal flow. Of course, what's ideal changes with the seasons of your life, too.

When Emily and I first moved from our one-bedroom apartment into this more spacious two-bedroom apartment, it felt like a palace. We decorated the narrow bonus room as a glorified gallery hallway with art. It was our own mini Metropolitan Museum of Art, though obviously with less valuable prints. We used the second bedroom—in what we humorously called the "East

Wing"—as a second living area, and dubbed it the "Reading Room." We got a used, bright yellow couch from friends, carried it nine blocks from their apartment to ours, and put together some bookshelves. We retreated to that quiet space in the evenings to read and escape the noise from the apartment of our elderly downstairs neighbor, who watched TV at a volume audible to everyone in the building, directly below our living room. The reading room was a happy luxury, perfect for that season of life.

When designing the shared spaces in your home, there is no more important guiding principle than paying attention to the rhythms and routines of *your* family.

Once we found out that we were pregnant with Mabel, however, we turned the reading room into a nursery, the art room into a playroom, and we went back to life with one living room (and a baby). When Matilda was born, Mabel got a roommate in her nursery. We quickly realized that Mabel couldn't play in the playroom or nursery while Matilda was napping. So we moved things around a little in the living room, ditched the ottoman because it took up precious floor space, and replaced our small white couch and two chairs with one long couch (in washable fabric—genius!). This gave Mabel more open space to play in the living area, and that room has continued to evolve as we've increased in numbers. Now our main living area serves as a living room, dining room, TV room, yoga studio, *and* play space.

Zoning Out

The year 2020 forever changed the way that many of us experience life in our homes. More people now work from home and find that having an "open plan"—which had been the popular architectural layout in new homes for years—isn't desirable anymore. Julia Marcum, the creator of one of my favorite Instagram accounts, "Chris Loves Julia," recently shared that she had closed off doorways and added walls in her North Carolina home to create a dedicated "dining room" and "home office," rather than keeping a more "open plan" layout. People on the internet were shocked, but they don't live there, her family does!

While most of us aren't handy enough to quickly add walls to our spaces, we *can* designate "zones" with furniture, rugs, cabinets, bookcases, and tables. Zones are a way to allocate the organizational real estate in your home by considering how the space is used. In the upcoming chapters we're going to apply the concept of zoning to various rooms in your home.

For now, let's start with shared living spaces. These spaces can be particularly tricky, because whether they are large or small, shared living spaces almost always have multiple uses, among them entertaining, lounging, dining, and playing. Considering the various ways that your family uses the space is a great first step toward determining what zones to establish in the space.

Our cottage in Pennsylvania has a living area that our real estate agent called a "great room." It is great—it's almost double the size of our apartment living area. But in some ways, the additional square footage made it even more of a puzzle to design and configure. There were so many options! The room is a long rectangle, and the previous owners, using two large rugs, divided the room into two distinct zones: dining and entertainment. A large couch divided the room in half, facing toward the wood-burning stove and television.

This layout worked for them, but Emily and I wanted to highlight what we considered to be the most beautiful feature of the room: the floor-to-ceiling windows that faced the great outdoors. We wanted to creatively rethink how to establish zones that worked for *us*. We also needed to consider how renters would use the space.

We market our cottage primarily to extended families who are gathering for long weekends in the mountains. We divided the large room into three zones instead of two, with a dining table, a four-person seating area with comfy chairs, and a couch located on a large rug with cabinets full of games, puzzles, and books. As with our NYC apartment, play space was one of our top priorities, so we skipped a coffee table and left the floor open for play. Although there is a television in the room, the overall space was designed to be oriented toward the windows. Movie nights are fun, but we knew our television wouldn't be on 24/7. We didn't buy a cottage in the Pocono Mountains to spend all our time watching television while we're there.

Assessing the ideal lifestyle we wanted from the cottage helped us to create zones that supported what we needed from the space. Whether you're thinking about creating zones for a city apartment, a mountain cottage, a country farmhouse, a sprawling suburb home, or a castle, here are some important considerations:

Zoning Shared Living Spaces

Lounge/Entertainment: In this zone, prioritize comfortable seating oriented around what you care about: the television, a coffee table, a game table, a window view, or a fireplace. Area rugs can help define this space and are also great for kids to play on. Storage ottomans can be helpful for housing games and toys and can also be used as footrests, extra seating, or places to set a drink. Since this area sees a lot of action in most homes, I'd recommend choosing furniture pieces in washable fabrics and/or that have cushion covers you can spot-clean or dry-clean.

Dining: Even if your floor plan has a room labeled "dining room," that might not be your priority for the space. You might consider flexible furniture options like a table that has leaves that can fold down or expand, or bench seating that allows you to tuck the seats under the table or move the benches to another part of the shared living space for additional seating options. It's always nice when one piece of furniture can serve multiple purposes!

Entrance/Exit: If your living area contains an entrance/exit door, consider how to add pieces to manage the items you inevitably have in your hands while coming in and out of the space. Hooks on the back of doors or on nearby walls can add storage for bags, keys, coats, and other accessories. Small cabinets with doors can also add storage without the visual clutter that can come from tossing your items down in the living area when you come in the door.

Play Area: Young kids often want to play in the same area as family members. Even if you keep toys in their bedrooms or have a designated playroom, you will probably also need to address the issue of zoning a play space within shared living areas. Baskets, carts, storage cabinets, or bookcases can all be helpful places to keep toys organized and contained, reduce visual clutter, and help kids find the things they want. An important note: Always remember to anchor bookcases or tall storage pieces to the walls.

Designing Shared Space for Your Rhythm

Getting out of the door to school on time used to be a major pain point for our family. I'd happily sing "Let's go, girls . . ." in true Shania Twain style, but the routine was tricky no matter how upbeat I was. We all had to find what we needed for the day and be dressed appropriately for the weather, and the clock was always ticking. For us, the foundation of a more successful getting-out-the-door routine was creating an organizational system that better complemented our morning rhythm. In our apartment, that means we reconfigured the space near the door. We used to have a beautiful table and standing lamp there, but decided to forgo elegance in favor of practicality. We brought in a three-level shoe tray, coat hooks, a cabinet with shelves that hold multiple clear bins for each person, a mirror, hooks for keys and bags, an organizer for mail, and a drop zone with a tray for wallets and sunglasses. It takes up the same amount of space as our old table and lamp, but is actually functional!

We also organized this area with our kids' eye level in mind. Our youngest daughter's bins are on the lowest shelves, so that even she can reach her things (like warm hats and gloves in the winter, or sun hats and sunglasses in the summer) independently. We installed the wall coat hooks at a low level so that all the girls can hang their jackets and backpacks by themselves.

Do we always get out the door on time? No. But is the process less stressful now? Yes.

That's a major win in my book.

We update the items in this area of our apartment seasonally, and once the station is set up for the new season, we take our girls on a tour and show them how and where things are organized. Our girls feel a sense of comfort when they know where their things are located, and they are better set up for success when they understand how the system works. They even provide input on things that would be helpful to have stored here—such as their socks for school. That small change means that they no longer have to run back to the bedroom to grab them!

Organizational Tips and Tricks
for Shared Living Spaces

The living area is where *so much life* happens, and in our experience, that also makes it a magnet for stuff to accumulate from other rooms in the home. Picture pajamas, baby dolls, craft supplies, snack cups, water bottles, ponytail holders, and homework. You name it, it finds its way onto the floor in our living room. It's a daily struggle to escort these things back to where they actually belong. Here are some of my favorite organizational tips and tricks for the living area:

1. **Catchall bin:** My grandma enjoys collecting antiques, and she gifted me one of her Longaberger baskets. It looks like a piece of art, but now this sentimental item serves an important purpose in our living room. At the end of the day I take the empty basket on a little "shopping trip" around our living room, scooping up all the small things that belong somewhere else in the home, and then carry them back to their designated spaces.

2. **Large baskets:** Large baskets can be a helpful way to group similar categories of items together. We use an open basket in our living room for extra blankets on movie nights. We also have a basket near our door, meaning our girls can walk into the apartment, unload their backpacks, and then place them in the basket so that they are easily found the next morning.

3. **Paper file:** It's easy to quickly accumulate a large pile of bills, catalogs, letters, shopping lists, to-do lists, art projects from school, and more, and sometimes that means that important stuff gets lost in the literal shuffle! We have a four-tier letter tray to organize four categories of paper: incoming, pending, outgoing, and art/sentimental. If we don't have time to deal with the piece of paper in question, we can just toss it into one of the four labeled trays and then deal with it by category later.

4. **Trays:** Flat surfaces can be clutter magnets! Trays help to zone and add physical barriers to flat surfaces such as coffee tables, end tables, and dining tables (plus kitchen counters, which we'll get to). They can also be helpful in the entryway for keys, cellphones, and other small items that clutter your pockets.

5. **Vertical storage:** Vertical spaces—the back of doors, the space over doorframes, the tops of bookcases, cabinets, and shelving units—can be prime organizational real estate. When selecting items to store in your highest vertical spaces, make sure to choose those that you don't frequently need to access. Our ice skates are in baskets on top of our living area cabinet, but you'd never know it. Also invest in a foldable step stool!

6. **Coat/bag hooks:** Vertical door hooks, compared with horizontal hooks, are able to hold a large volume of coats and bags, and help create a system that makes it easy to

"grab and go." We added two long vertical hooks that each feature five hanging prongs to the back of our living room door. We also added a low layer of hooks at the perfect height for our girls to use to independently grab their coats. When kids have access to the things that they need, they're much less likely to ask you to get things for them. That's a win-win!

7. **Storage seating:** Consider how you could use seating alternatives to double as storage options in your living area. At our cottage, we use multipurpose ottomans as storage, seating, and footrests, and as a coffee table alternative. In our apartment dining zone, we swapped a few of our kitchen chairs for bench seating. The benches have open cubby space beneath the seats, and we were able to add storage baskets inside. Since this storage area is located near our entryway door, we use these baskets to store additional shoes.

8. **Closet organization:** Closets are a precious resource! It's important to maximize their organization to serve a specific function for your household. If you have a closet in your living area, it could be used to store games and puzzles, to keep extra blankets for movie nights, or to house extra dining room items, like platters and serving bowls. It could also serve as a getting-out-the-door area, with storage for coats and bags. Think about your needs for the space, create an organizational map, and don't let it become a catchall zone.

9. **Technology bin:** Technology items come with so many cords, which can be difficult to contain without their becoming tangled. But if Rapunzel can tame her locks, you can tame your cords. You don't need to rush out to purchase a fancy cord-containing system or special tech storage dividers. You can take a basket, add in smaller containers, and then partition items so that you can grab what you need when you need it! Also, after you head to the store for that new tech device, make sure to declutter those old cords, chargers, screen protectors, etc. Old tech can be fun to look back on in a museum, but it doesn't need to clutter your space!

10. **Shoe storage:** It's time to *stop wearing your shoes in your house.* Shoes are filthy! Think about all the places where you step each day, and if you're in a bigger city, just think about *everything* that happens on the sidewalks. It's disgusting. Shoe storage racks provide multiple levels of storage, and trays can catch the wet drips from your shoes on rainy or snowy days.

Shared Spaces with Kids

When you're sharing a space with children, there are two categories of items that are important to distinguish—items you *want* your children to be able to access independently and items that you *don't want* your children to be able to access independently.

Frankly, there's also a third category: items that you wish your children would never play with again but that just keep showing up, like glitter, slime, and nonwashable markers. When designing organizational systems for kids, those category considerations should be at the forefront of your mind.

Toy Rotation System

Our toy rotation closet is the center jewel in our organizational crown. It's almost as Insta-famous as my tiny bedroom closet. It's directly off our kitchen (most people would call it a pantry) and is the four-by-four-foot space where we store toys, activities, workbooks, and art supplies. We established the toy rotation closet for several reasons. Our playroom is narrow, so we wanted to limit the amount of toys in the space at any given time, to make sure the floor space was easy to walk through and leave plenty of open space for play. We wanted the girls to have access to their toys, but they didn't need *all* of them out *all* of the time. We wanted to give them choice, set up new play experiences, and keep toys feeling fresh. If you want to create a toy rotation system in your home, you don't necessarily have to give up your pantry. You could create a similar system in a section of any closet, in a bookshelf, in a dresser, or even using storage containers stacked in an extra space like a basement, attic, or garage.

To make our toy rotation system work, we cleared space in our kitchen pantry (more on this in chapter 8) and completed a toy inventory. It's a process that we've had to repeat multiple times—remember, decluttering isn't a onetime event—but it's made all

Grandparent Gifts

My mom's love language is gift-giving, and one of her thoughtful ideas actually landed us on *Good Morning America*. Several years ago for Christmas at my mom's, she gifted Mabel and Matilda each a doll with lots of clothes and accessories. The dolls were too large to fit in our carry-on bags for our return flight, so my mom said the dolls could live with her in Kentucky. Audrey Anne and Bonnie Rose became special "Nana" dolls, and they come with her to NYC each time she visits. The girls are always excited to see their doll friends and Emily and I love that all the doll accessories and gear go back home with Nana.

A *GMA* producer caught wind of the story of the dolls, and we were featured in a segment about how families stay connected despite distance. A film crew was sent to my mom's house in Kentucky, and another film crew was sent to our apartment, and virtually we filmed a segment together.

Several weeks later, our family was invited to the studio to help introduce the segment. After a brief introduction, who walked out through the hidden door in a storm of confetti? My mom, aka Nana, holding Audrey Anne and Bonnie Rose. It was such an epic surprise, and reinforced the ingenious idea of keeping grandparents' gifts at grandparents' houses! Playing with toys that are kept at grandparents' houses is another way to experience the joy of a toy rotation.

the difference. To inventory toys, I recommend that you gather all the toys from every room in your home into a central location, assess what you see (it's likely to be a mountain of things), then sort the items into categories and edit.

We refer to this project as "The Great Toy Edit," and we complete it twice a year, before the holidays and before the birthday season. This is always an epic project, and once it starts there's the feeling of "Mid-Project Regret Syndrome," a phrase coined by Susie Allison of the online parenting account "Busy Toddler." Things always get worse before they get better. This project invites you to choose what to keep, what to move out, and to then create a plan for how to organize it all.

Emily's expertise in pediatric occupational therapy has profoundly enriched my understanding of how children acquire developmental skills through interaction with toys across various categories. Her insights have been invaluable in guiding our selection of toys for the girls. It's easy to be overwhelmed before an upcoming gift-giving occasion by the thought of more toys coming into your home. It can be helpful to assess what toys you already have, and then consider which of the following toy categories you might want to potentially bring additional items in to (and then *gently* guide gift-givers). We try to prioritize toys that align with current interests and facilitate progression toward more advanced levels of play and learning.

Toy Inventory Categories

- **Imaginative:** Nearly all categories of toys can be incorporated into imaginative play, but some specific items that help facilitate this include a play kitchen with play food and accessories, a grocery cart and cash register, baby dolls with a stroller, animal puppets, dress-up clothes, and accessories for imaginative occupation-based play, like a doctor kit. These things help set a scene, but don't dictate the play itself.

- **Building:** Different types of block sets work on different fine motor skills. A wooden block set is perfect for teaching kids how to balance items on top of one another. Wooden blocks can be used to practice stacking, balancing, and building towers. Interlocking blocks (Mega Bloks, Bristle Blocks, LEGOs) require pushing the pieces together. Magnetic blocks can connect in lots of different ways and are another way to practice eye-hand coordination. A marble run construction set is a fun way for older kids to expand their building skills.

- **Vehicles:** A road rug mat, road tape, or interlocking or magnetic street pieces are fun ways to add a visual element to vehicle play with toy cars and trucks. A set of wooden traffic signs and a set of characters can be used to expand this play into a city or neighborhood.

- **Arts and Crafts:** There are so many items that can fall into this category. It can be helpful to keep a variety of art supplies like construction paper, coloring books, stickers, stamps and ink pads, markers, crayons, and colored pencils in one designated area or in a three-tier cart that can be rolled over to a table. Other items that you want your kids to use with more supervision (paints, glitter, and scissors immediately come to mind!) can be stored in a separate bin that is less accessible. You could also use an elastic tablecloth to protect the table.

- **Fine Motor:** It's important to have a variety of toys that allow kids to stack, sort, push, and pull with their fingers, to build their fine motor skills. Fine motor toys include things like shape sorters, ring stackers, Potato Heads, lacing beads, and tools that allow them to coordinate their fingers to pick things up and transfer them, like tongs, tweezers, and droppers.

- **Puzzles:** Young kids can start inserting peg puzzles into a board, and then gradually progress to twelve pieces, twenty-four pieces, forty-eight pieces, and more. There are small table puzzles and large floor puzzles, and also puzzle racks to help keep puzzles organized in a closet or on a shelf. It's a great way to build visual problem-solving.

- **Instruments:** From a toddler's xylophone, tap drum, rainmaker stick, and maracas set to an older kid's wooden ukulele, recorder, keyboard, and karaoke machine, there are lots of options available to let children experience the joy of creating and listening to music. But buyer beware of a full-on drum set!

- **Sensory:** A sensory bin can be an enjoyable way to expose children to different textures. They can be filled with water, sand, rice, beans, shaving cream, cotton balls, and more. There are also sensory activities that can be enjoyed at a table with fine motor tools, like Play-Doh, play foam, and slime—although your kids may need to be highly supervised.

- **Gross Motor:** Having a few gross motor toys available for indoor play can help when kids are inside but need to move their bodies! A tunnel or ball pit set (which can both collapse and store flat) can be a fun indoor activity for younger kids to crawl through. Older kids might enjoy practicing yoga on a fold-up play mat, learning gymnastic moves on a foldable balance beam, or walking across balance stepping stones. A wooden climbing triangle and a soft modular foam play couch can entertain kids for years.

Speaking of Filth

"Tidy Dad, do your kids ever create messes?" The simple answer is no. My children are perfectly well-behaved little robots who always do as I ask and never *ever* create a mess. They also never color outside of the lines. We're so #blessed.

In reality, dealing with the mess of life with children is a universal equalizer in parenting circles. Watching our little walking tornadoes in action can feel overwhelming. They're so fast. And so destructive.

Our girls love to create art, love to play, and love to make creative little messes. As they should . . . They're kids! Our dining room table is one of their favorite places to create and play. It is large enough for them to pull out their three-tier art cart from the toy rotation, spread out all their materials, and sit around the table together. Before all the art supplies come out, I put down a waterproof, washable elastic tablecloth. It fits securely over the edges of the table and acts as a water-and-marker-proof barrier. It protects the table when the girls are drawing, coloring, cutting with scissors, gluing, and painting. If the tablecloth gets colored on or painted on, I just take it off and throw it in the washing machine. It's also super helpful when the girls craft with beads or small pieces. Instead of picking up the pieces one by one when they're done working on the project, I can just remove the tablecloth and funnel all the pieces into a storage box for the next time.

Our dining table sees a lot of messes, as does the rest of our living area. Let's talk about the "Dirty Dozen" of the living area.

Living Area Dirty Dozen

1. **Underneath area rugs:** Most people regularly vacuum their living room rugs, but when was the last time you cleaned the floors underneath? I encourage you to remove any small pieces of furniture that are sitting on the rug and gently roll back one side. Sweep, vacuum, and mop the uncovered floor space before rolling the rug back down, then repeat the process on the other side. Here's a bonus tip to extend your rug's lifespan: Rotate it quarterly. This

helps to distribute wear and tear more evenly, and also gives you a regular rhythm to remembering to clean underneath it!

2. **Underneath couch cushions:** Before you start vacuuming, remember to fully remove the cushions—no shortcuts here! To elevate your cleaning game, try placing your robot vacuum on the couch frame while the cushions are off. Its sensors will prevent any mishaps, and it'll efficiently tackle leftover crumbs and debris. And don't forget: Give those hardworking cushions a thorough wash periodically to extend the lifespan of your sofa. Be sure to follow the manufacturer's recommendations for best results.

3. **Baseboards behind furniture:** Baseboards are dust magnets of epic proportions. Experience the satisfaction of pulling your furniture away from the wall, grabbing a damp cloth, and banishing dust and grime. For extra dust-fighting power, follow up by wiping the baseboards with a dryer sheet. This helps create a dust-repellent barrier.

4. **Ceiling fan blades:** Despite their constant motion, these are dust magnets, too, but you can combat buildup easily with a few sprays of multipurpose cleaner and a microfiber cloth. Alternatively, use this clever hack: Wrap a pillowcase around each blade, gently pulling it toward you to trap dust inside. Flip the pillowcase inside out to dispose of dust, then toss it in the laundry for a fresh start.

5. **Lampshades:** For lampshade cleaning, a lint roller is your ultimate ally. Pro tip: Keep the dusty lint roller strip on afterward, and then remove it right before the next use, so that you're starting with a dust-free one each time.

6. **Windows:** For streak-free windows in any room, try using newspapers, microfiber towels, or coffee filters—they're gentle and effective. Dish soap and warm water work just as well as glass cleaner. Remember to clean the inside of windows with horizontal strokes and the outside with vertical strokes to minimize streaks. And don't forget the windowsills! You can use a pressurized steam cleaner for stubborn dirt and debris.

7. **Filters:** Regularly cleaning the filter is crucial for all air circulation systems, whether it's a window unit, central AC, HVAC, or air purifier. Some units require quarterly replacement of filters, while others have washable or vacuumable filters. Set a reminder to check them!

8. **Doorknobs and handles:** When I was growing up, my mom, who worked in a hospital laboratory, introduced me to a fascinating science experiment: uncovering the dirtiest spots in our house. We'd swab various surfaces, transfer the samples to petri dishes, and observe the bacteria growth under microscopes. Without fail, doorknobs and handles proved to be shockingly dirty! This experience left a lasting impression, and now, as an adult, I diligently disinfect our doorknobs and handles with a disinfectant cleaner and

rag. I also emphasize the importance of frequent hand-washing to my family.

9. **Underneath tables:** The underside of tables can accumulate hidden dirt and grime, especially if napkins aren't provided with every meal. If you're up for it, get down on your knees or lie on your back to tackle this task. Armed with a rag and some cleaner, engage in a satisfying deep cleaning session. Alternatively, enlist the help of your kids to get the job done!

10. **Tech gear:** Our tech gear is constantly by our side, but let's face it—they're often filthy little devices! In the living room, you may think about cleaning remote controls, but don't forget about any cellphones, tablets, e-readers, and smartwatches. I prefer to gently spray a microfiber cloth with a disinfectant cleaning solution and wipe down the surfaces of these devices. Warm, soapy water can also work as a safe and gentle cleaner. Just remember to follow up with a dry cloth. Tech and water don't mix!

11. **Window blinds, curtains, and shades:** More dust magnets! I have vivid memories of my mom putting our plastic blinds in the bathtub with some soap to clean the dust off the individual blades. That method does work, but you can also vacuum blinds and shades, and most curtains are machine-washable or suitable for dry cleaning. Just be sure to check the fabric tag for the recommended cleaning instructions.

12. **Picture frames:** Picture frames in our living room are *usually* in need of both updating and cleaning. To begin, remove the photos and separate the glass from the frame. Then, use a microfiber cloth to dust the frame, followed by window cleaner to wipe the glass. This simple process will ensure that your photos shine beautifully once again.

INDEPENDENT PRACTICE

Sketch It Out

It's time to embrace your inner HGTV Design Star and envision the potential of your shared living spaces. Whether it's creating a serene reading nook or a lively entertainment area, let your imagination run wild. By unleashing your creativity and carefully considering your goals, challenges, and potential configurations, you'll be well on your way to transforming your shared living spaces into inviting and functional havens that reflect your family's unique lifestyle.

1. **Goals for the space:** Describe your ideal lifestyle in the room. Do you envision cozy gatherings with friends, peaceful evenings curled up with a book, or perhaps a multifunctional space that accommodates both work and play?

2. **Design challenges:** Consider any obstacles or constraints in the space. Are there awkward corners, limited natural light, or existing furniture arrangements that need to be

worked around? Addressing these challenges up-front will help you create a functional and visually appealing layout.

3. **Zone it out:** Explore different configurations for the space. Sketch out various layouts, experimenting with furniture placement and zoning. Identify what you like and don't like about each plan, considering factors such as flow, accessibility, and aesthetic appeal.

4. **Try it out:** Take action to bring your vision to life. Begin by moving furniture around to test different layouts. Get creative with decor and accessories to enhance each zone's ambiance. Don't be afraid to mix and match pieces from different areas of your home to achieve the desired look and feel.

8

Organizing Your Kitchen Like a Master Chef

As the saying goes, "The kitchen is the heart of the home," where daily life converges, from meal preparation to messy cleanups to family gatherings. Consider how to embrace innovative organization solutions to simplify mealtime routines, ensuring flow, efficiency, and joy.

One of my favorite photos from when we were parents to just one bubbly, bouncing little baby named Mabel shows Emily and me sitting at our kitchen table. We're drinking cups of tea, little Mabel is sitting on Emily's lap, and we're looking at one of her sonogram photos. The moment captures such a seemingly simple time in our lives when we had a little table for two that could comfortably fit in our kitchen.

By New York City standards, we had a generous galley-style kitchen with a large walk-in pantry where we stored our food, small appliances, and cleaning supplies. It measured four feet by four feet, and we often joked that our pantry was the size of most NYC nurseries.

At that time, Mabel was a tiny, immobile being who occupied lots of our mental and emotional energy, but very little physical real estate. Up until that point, she'd never made a food mess or tried to cook eggs for herself. That reality flew straight out the window when she turned six months old and started joining us at the table. She *loved* food and smearing it all over herself and anyone or anything within reach.

Now we faced a dilemma: Where to put Messy Mabel's high chair? When we put it at our table, it blocked the walkway between the table and the counters and oven, which meant we could no longer comfortably move through our kitchen. The walls felt like they were closing in, and something had to give.

Emily came up with the idea of moving the table into the corner of the living area to allow Mabel to comfortably sit with us. We sold a few chairs, ditched the ottoman, and relocated the television to a different wall. Then we moved our kitchen table into the newly available living room corner.

This opened up valuable space in the kitchen to add a storage hutch and open shelving, which created more space for meal prep and storage. We were then able to move items from our kitchen pantry into the new storage, which opened up space in our pantry. We used that space to move some toys from the playroom into the pantry closet and created a toy rotation, which created more open space in the playroom for play. Emily's idea resulted in a great domino effect!

How We Made Sense of the Mess and Determined What Was "Just Enough"

Seeing the domino effect play out was really exciting, but making sense of how to relocate things within the kitchen took work. As we unloaded things from our cabinets, we realized that the organization of items definitely wasn't intuitive and had created several clutter traps. Our "out of sight, out of mind" organizational philosophy was on full display. We found items we had rarely or never used. It was clear we'd made the common mistake when we moved in of simply "putting things wherever they fit." So, we unloaded everything from the cabinets, drawers, baskets, and bins into our living room as our staging ground for sorting and assessing. We discovered that we had two major categories of items: our everyday items and our infrequently used items.

If you haven't confronted any excess that may exist in your kitchen, organizing it all will be overwhelming.

If you haven't confronted any excess that may exist in your kitchen, organizing it all will be overwhelming. Dealing with the excess can lead to answering the question of "What is just enough?" That answer is essential to establishing a kitchen that works *for* you and not *against* you!

Variety is the spice of life, but if you have a small kitchen, you need to be incredibly ruthless about the volume of that spice. Here are some common categories of kitchen items that you may want to consider decluttering:

Declutter *This*: Kitchen Edition

1. **Kitchen towels:** I'm personally looking for a towel that is absorbent, quick drying, and able to handle spills and stains of all color varieties. I don't need ones with inspirational quotes or pictures of places I've traveled. You may have different criteria, and that's okay! In terms of numbers, I think that having a three-to-five-day supply is plenty—enough to get through one week, and then we wash them!

2. **Casserole dishes:** Who doesn't love a good casserole that consists of previously frozen veggies, a little cheddar cheese, and a can of cream of chicken soup? Hey, don't knock it until you try it! But in all seriousness, I think no one really needs more casserole dishes than can all fit in the oven at one time. If you have a friend in need and want to provide a meal, you can skip the casserole and send them a gift card to order takeout.

3. **Coffee mugs:** It is indeed possible for one family to have too many! These can be a fun item to collect, but it is also possible for them to quickly become a clutter trap. Decide how much space you want to allocate to mugs—a cabinet,

a shelf, an area by the coffeepot? You may need to decide how many mugs to keep based on how many can actually fit in your preferred location.

4. **Themed party supplies:** There's definitely a market out there for themed party supply items, and I think my mom *is* that market. She loves throwing "cheap but fabulous" parties with specialty cocktails, her latest Pinterest snack creation, and themed decor. She has lots of colorful party glasses, themed platters and trays, and novelty drink toppers for summer pool parties. I love attending her parties, but don't share the same affinity, or space, for storing novelty items.

5. **Specialty kitchen gadgets:** It's okay to make space for specialty kitchen gadgets if you use them regularly and they bring you joy. But if you don't actually use them, let them go! I'm talking about those kitchen tools that only serve *one* purpose: an avocado slicer, a strawberry stem huller, an apple corer . . . Those cutting tasks could all be replaced with a kitchen knife instead.

6. **Food storage containers:** If it doesn't have a lid, it's time for it to go. If it can't be refrigerated, frozen, and micro-waved, it can go. Need I say more? Pro tip: We also store some empty food storage containers in the refrigerator. This ensures we always have room for leftovers.

It's Okay to Get Sentimental

We have kept some things that we love even if we don't use them all the time. And that's okay—they are uniquely interesting and special to *us*. For example, we have an extensive collection of cookie cutters, which my mom adds to each holiday season. I also have a small "Queen and Corgi" set of salt and pepper shakers that rest on the magnetic shelf attached to the side of our refrigerator. Each day as I'm making my morning cup of coffee, they warmly greet me. They both bring me so much joy.

Emily's late grandmother's china is another example. Her grandmother gifted us the dishes when we got married, and we had them stored safely in a box for several years, unused and wrapped in protective paper. Stemming from Emily's domino-effect brainstorm, we added floating shelves in our kitchen and pulled the dishes out of storage to display them on the shelves. Now we use them regularly for "special" meals, like birthdays, holidays, or even princess tea parties with the girls. They love eating and drinking from the special dishes!

What sentimental items do you have stored away that you could display or use in your daily life? It's time to bring them out.

Cooking Up Kitchen Efficiency with Clever Zoning

The kitchen is the heart of the home. So much life happens in a relatively small space. Snack times, mealtimes, prepping for

Unpacking with a Plan

It's exciting to move into a new place! But once the truck is unloaded and you see the mountain of boxes before you, the feeling of euphoria can quickly fade. It's easy to feel overwhelmed, and the urgency kicks in to unpack, put away items, and remove those boxes from sight as soon as possible! I invite you to consider the idea of "unpacking with a plan." If you can come to terms with the fact that a "moving mess" is unavoidable, you can step back and take the time to develop a strategic organizational plan to facilitate where things are going to be stored. Sketch out your plans, draw a map, and invite the people you live with to consider how best to allocate organizational real estate. *Then* put things away!

meals, cleaning up after meals. Likewise, so much joy comes from being able to find the kitchen gadgets that you need, precisely when you need them! After unloading our kitchen and decluttering items, we were incredibly excited to draw blueprint plans and set up a zoning system.

Emily and I initially learned of the concept of "kitchen zoning" from Cook Smarts, a meal planning service that we've used for years as part of our mealtime surthrival strategy. In addition to publishing amazing recipes and user-friendly cooking guides, Cook Smarts founder Jess Dang also publishes resources designed to help make working in the kitchen less stressful and more joyous. We discovered her article on "Kitchen Zoning" around the same time that we were inspired to declutter and reorganize our small kitchen. It's beautiful when the right resources find their way into your hands at the right time!

The concept of kitchen zoning is that everything gets organized by category and stored in the location where it is used most often. As Jess said in the article, "Your goal is to have someone else use your kitchen and easily find everything because your placement of items would feel so intuitive." Jess recommends four zones for every kitchen, and we've added a fifth: a dedicated kid zone. Here are our five kitchen zones and a list of items that could be stored in each zone:

Kitchen Zone	Items in Zone
Prep Zone: area where you prep ingredients for cooking	cutting board, knives, spices, vinegars, oils, peelers, measuring cups, measuring spoons, kitchen scale, colander, mixing bowls, grater, garlic press, zester, slicer, choppers, can opener
Cooking Zone: area where most cooking happens	pots, pans, Dutch oven, wok, tongs, spatulas, wooden spoons, whisk, meat thermometer, baking items, small appliances
Cleanup Zone: area around your sink and dishwasher	drying rack, drying mat, dish soap, sponges, washcloths, rags, kitchen towels, kitchen cleaning supplies, trash bags

Kitchen Zone	Items in Zone
Putting-Away Zone: area between your cleanup zone and refrigerator	plates, bowls, glasses, utensils, serving ware, tinfoil, plastic wrap, bag clips, food huggers, food storage containers
Kid Zone: area accessible to your kids	kid-friendly plates, utensils, napkins, cups, water bottles, straws, bowls, snack containers, food storage containers

We took this idea to heart. Emily and I sketched out a map of the kitchen that included all the cabinets, drawers, and counter space. We identified the locations for our five kitchen zones: a prep zone, a cooking zone, a cleanup zone, a putting-away zone, and a kid zone. Next, we sorted the mountain of kitchen items into each of those five categories to further assess what we wanted to keep and what we wanted to move out.

Meal prepping used to look like opening one cabinet to pull out the cutting board and walking it over next to the knives, then walking to the far side of the kitchen to pull out the ingredients, then reaching into the back of a cabinet to pull out containers to store the prepped ingredients. Zoning our kitchen gave us a strategic plan for how to allocate real estate in our kitchen in an intuitive way. Now our cutting board and knives are stored on the surface directly next to our refrigerator, so that we can pull out veggies, chop them, and then put them away. It has made the cooking process so much more efficient.

Pro Tip: Cabinet Decor

The inside of cabinet doors can be a great place to store kids' artwork, sentimental cards, or paper mementos. Don't think of this as hiding these things, but rather as giving yourself a nice little surprise every time you open the cabinet. It's a beautiful thing to open a cabinet door and be reminded of a time of importance or significance or value. Every time I open the spice cabinet, I see Mabel's preschool handprint next to the words "Mom and Dad." If not for this display location on the back of the cabinet door, it would likely be stored away in her art file. I love that I'm able to see and enjoy her artwork every day!

Getting Organized

Once you've earmarked items for a particular zone, it's time to consider how to organize items *within* the zones. As you move items back in, resist the urge to simply stack them on shelves. This is an opportunity to think creatively about how to organize your kitchen so that you and the people you live with can easily access the things that are needed for mealtimes. Here are some items that can help you organize your kitchen. Consider what could work in your space.

1. **Add magnetic baskets to the refrigerator.** In most kitchens, the refrigerator is in close proximity to the prep zone,

and the sides of many refrigerators are magnetic, making them the perfect blank canvas for organization. Magnetic baskets can be a great option for storing items that you want easily accessible. We have a magnetic basket that stores two canisters for coffee and sugar, in addition to our most commonly used spices like salt, pepper, cinnamon, and everything-bagel seasoning.

2. **Use stackable countertop shelves.** Counters are a valuable resource in a kitchen, but can easily become cluttered. Consider using stackable countertop shelves to help you organize items. Shelves can be stacked on top of one another or lined up side by side to create multiple smaller levels of storage.

3. **Store produce in baskets.** Stackable or hanging baskets can be a great option for fruits and vegetables. Some baskets also include adjustable dividers to help you neatly separate your produce and built-in handles to make carrying easier. Look for containers with slats in the sides to allow for proper air circulation, which helps to keep your fruits and vegetables fresh for longer.

4. **Invest in a spice rack.** Chefs recommend that spices you use often be stored in glass or tin containers, in a dark cabinet or drawer, which helps them remain pungent. Spices that are used less frequently can be stored in the freezer. Investing in same-sized glass spice jars keeps your spices fresh, and they can be organized in a drawer or in a rack in a cabinet. Label your spices so you don't mix up

the paprika with the cinnamon. (I'm speaking from experience here.) Also keep a collapsible funnel nearby so you can add additional spices to a jar when it's running low. We keep our back stock behind the spice rack on the same cabinet shelf, so that storing our spice rack plus extra spices doesn't take up any additional space.

5. **Use clear bins as "drawers."** Our kitchen has only three drawers! We now treat bins like "drawers" and use them to organize small categories of items such as snacks, fruit, seasoning packets, tea bags, and more. Look for sets with removable dividers. Bins are very versatile and can be used inside a refrigerator, pantry, or cabinet.

6. **Add baskets to the top of cabinets.** If your cabinets don't go all the way to the ceiling, then consider adding baskets on top for additional storage. Baskets can be a great place to store seasonal cooking items, pantry back stock, or your stash of secret snacks that you eat when the children are tucked into their beds for the night. For added ease, look for baskets with handles that you can face toward where you'll need to grab them.

7. **Add turntables to tricky kitchen spaces.** Commonly referred to as "lazy Susans," these are another incredibly versatile organizational product. I find that they are particularly handy in awkward corner cabinets and can also be useful for storing condiments in the refrigerator. Turntables allow you to access many different products

without having to move all the items to get the one in the back!

8. **Add hooks to the inside of cabinets.** The inside of a cabinet door can be a great place to add a hook and hang pot holders or oven mitts. A hook on the inside of the door of the cabinet near the sink can be used to hang rags, kitchen towels, or sponges.

9. **Install wall shelving.** Shelves can provide valuable storage and can help you create grab-and-go systems. When we added open shelving to our kitchen, we decided to display our colorful plates and bowls, which makes it easy to grab those items and set the table without opening and closing cabinet doors. If you have beautiful plates or serving ware, consider how to artfully arrange and organize those items for easy access.

10. **Add pull-out cabinet drawers and baskets to deep cabinets.** If your kitchen cabinets are deep, adding baskets or sliding drawers that you can pull out will be really useful. This is a way to create different levels of storage, and will make it so much easier to access things stored in the back of cabinets. We also added a pull-out drawer to the cabinet under the kitchen sink. This is a great spot to store kitchen cleaning supplies.

11. **Utilize tiered storage options.** Carts, stackable drawers, and freestanding shelving units can help to provide

additional storage. These units help to utilize vertical space, creating multiple tiers of storage in the same area.

12. **Invest in uniform lids for food storage containers.** Food storage containers that have different-sized lids are a nightmare. We recently discovered a set of containers that features containers in four different sizes, but they all have the *same*-sized lid. It's been a game changer. It's easy to grab one lid and put it on whichever container we're using.

13. **Go vertical with canned goods.** Organizing canned goods into a tiered storage rack can keep them neatly organized while simultaneously maximizing your space.

14. **Use clear baskets inside cabinets.** It can be helpful to use baskets inside of cabinets to contain small items by category. The entire basket can be pulled down, rather than your having to rummage through loose items on a cabinet shelf.

15. **Take advantage of doors.** The front and back of doors can be valuable storage spaces. There are a variety of over-the-door organizers that are easy to install, and you can add hooks, baskets, or shelves to either your cabinet doors or full-sized doors utilizing these otherwise unused spaces.

To Decant or Not to Decant

Decanting means emptying pantry items from their original packaging—pasta, oats, gumballs, whatever!—and then storing them in clear containers. I've discovered that it is a highly controversial issue in organizing circles.

Decanting is a system that has to be regularly maintained, and takes a few extra steps. Rather than tossing a bag of pretzels in the cabinet, you have to open the bag, open a container, pour the pretzels into the container, and hope that there are not too many pretzels to fit inside. Decanting certain items can be helpful, because you can quickly assess the quantity of food left in each container, foods have a longer shelf life when stored in airtight containers, and you can easily stack containers on shelves and see each item.

But there are pros and cons! We have done a much better job of maintaining this system for items like baking ingredients and dry-goods staples than for snacks we stock up on (and access) more frequently. Bottom line: Decanting looks nice, but might not always feel practical.

Cleanup in Aisle Seven

Once when my back was turned to them, our girls managed to pick up and subsequently drop on the kitchen floor the strawberry-watermelon smoothie that I'd just blended to cool us all down on a humid July afternoon. I saw the blender tumble in slow motion, and then the sticky mess was everywhere. The kitchen looked like a crime scene.

In New York City, city health inspectors assign letter grades to restaurants, which are then posted in the window directly next to the door of the restaurant for patrons to see. I don't eat anywhere that has lower than an A rating, and I often think of this grading system when tackling my own kitchen. The health inspector would surely check the Dirty Dozen and then give me an A.

I got on my hands and knees, grabbed an entire roll of paper towels, and began collecting remnants of the smoothie mixture into a bucket. Margaret grabbed a straw to suck the puddle off the floor; she wasn't letting that smoothie go to waste. Once the majority of the smoothie was off the floor, I mixed together a combination of dish soap, floor cleaner, and warm water to try and get the remaining sticky film of strawberry and watermelon off the floor. I had to scrub, empty the water, re-create the soap combination, and scrub again three separate times. Here's what I wish I'd known then: Using a wet/dry vacuum would have made all the difference!

How many times has your kid spilled milk PLUS cereal at the exact same moment? Mine do this all the time! Now I pull the wet/dry vacuum out of the base and quickly eliminate the sticky mixture. It literally sucks up liquid and solids *at the same time,* and then simultaneously mops the floor with clean water while holding the dirty water in a separate tank. I think they should send one of these to every new parent when they have a baby.

Speaking of dirty kitchen messes, let's take a look at the "Kitchen Dirty Dozen," twelve areas that require just a little more elbow grease, but are important to clean regularly.

Kitchen Dirty Dozen

1. **Under the refrigerator:** This area is a dust and crumb magnet. You can clean underneath it by gently pulling the refrigerator forward (please protect your floors) so that you're able to access the floor directly underneath where it's been standing. Some refrigerators are on rollers and others can be pulled forward by shimmying a towel under the front legs. If you've gone to all this trouble, be sure to both sweep and mop this area. Give the baseboards a good wash, and also wipe down the walls. I recommend using a microfiber cloth to gently wipe the back and sides of the refrigerator, removing any dust. If you have a problem with bugs, mice, or other unwanted creatures, this is a good opportunity to put down a few traps or insect sticky boards before pushing the fridge back into place.

2. **Refrigerator interior:** I like to start by wiping down the sides and bottom of the interior and then washing out the baskets, shelves, and bins in the bathtub! When cleaning the refrigerator, it's important to read the labels of the

Birthday Baking

Here's a little-known Tidy Dad fact: I have auditioned for half a dozen different baking shows, and have even made it to the final rounds of auditions twice; evidently, dad bakers of a certain age are underrepresented in casting circles. Every spring when I start to post photos and videos of the birthday cakes that I bake for the girls, the casting directors start to come out of the woodwork. I always happily entertain their requests—fill out their forms, submit casting videos, and set my sights on finally making my baking show debut. I think I'd be a great baking show guest. I'd bring the energy, the drama, and the tears.

As I've shared with casting directors, one of our favorite family traditions is collaborating on "Birthday Bakes." Each girl gets to design her own birthday cake, complete with toppings, flavors, and decorations, and then I bring them to life(ish). Over the years I've created Barbie cakes, spider cakes, unicorn cakes, caterpillar cakes, flowerpot cakes, and more! In my collection of sentimental papers, I've kept the beautifully illustrated plans that the girls have drawn up for me. On their birthdays, I find it's the cake that the girls look forward to most. Not the presents, not the party, but the moment when they finally see their creative designs come to life!

cleaning product you're using to see any specific safety considerations, since they'll be close to food. After using any cleaning product, I also generously wipe down the areas that have just been cleaned with a mixture of dish soap and warm water. Pro tip: Do this cleaning task the day before you leave for vacation—that's when the fridge is likely to be at its emptiest. Plus, it's so nice to come back to a clean fridge!

3. **Under the stove:** The stove can be slid forward in a similar method described for moving the refrigerator. An important additional note: Take extreme care with any gas lines or electric cords when pulling out the stove!

4. **Sides of stove:** This area is notoriously dirty, grimy, and neglected, so when you move the stove to clean underneath it, clean the sides before you push it back in. You can also add washable gap covers to the space between the stove and counters to prevent crumbs and spills from making their way down onto the sides of the stove.

5. **Stove hood/air vent:** The stove hood/air vent helps circulate air while you're cooking, but it also attracts dust and grease. Using steel wool, a strong grease-fighting cleaner (like dish soap), hot water, and a microfiber cloth can help you achieve a thorough cleaning and cut through any stuck-on gunk. Many stove hoods or vents also have a built-in light. Be sure to take the bulb out and give it a good degreasing as well.

6. **Tops of cabinets:** Just as heat rises, grease rises—and where do you think it lands? Yep, on top of the kitchen cabinets, and then dust particles undoubtedly follow. The result is a sticky, dusty mess. If you've never cleaned the top of your cabinets, you're in for an amazingly epic "before and after" cleaning experience. A hard sponge or brush and a dish soap/warm water mixture can help you lift away the grease and dust. Once the area is clean and dry, line the top of your cabinets with paper towels or newspaper. That will make cleaning it next time so much easier!

7. **Ceiling fan/light fixtures:** These can be notoriously tricky to clean, because grease can collect on the fixtures, becoming a magnet for dust. Turn off the light to let the light fixture and bulbs cool, and then you can unscrew the bulb and get it clean. You might also be able to take down part of the light fixture. If you can, run it under warm water and then wipe it clean. Afterward, your kitchen is going to shine (literally!) and it's going to be so much easier to see what you're doing.

8. **Bottoms of cabinets:** When there's a spill in the kitchen, where does the liquid go? Often onto the bottom of your cabinets or to the kickplate that connects your cabinet to your floor. These surfaces can be wiped clean with a microfiber cloth and water or any multisurface cleaner.

9. **Trash can:** The trash can is to the kitchen what the toilet bowl is to the bathroom. It sees so much dirty action and

therefore demands regular attention. If you have a yard, take your trash can to the great outdoors, add a bit of dish soap to the base, and then spray it clean with water (you can use a hose!). If you're like us and don't have outdoor space, take it to the bathroom and clean it in the tub. And then clean your bathtub afterward!

10. **Microwave interior:** This small yet mighty kitchen appliance can go from clean to filthy in less than ten seconds. If you need to remove stuck-on food particles, grease, and gunk, I recommend mixing a third of a cup of white distilled vinegar and a couple of inches of water in a coffee mug. Place the mug in the microwave and heat for one minute—this basically gives the microwave a little steam clean. Then remove the mug and use a microfiber cloth to wipe down the inside of the appliance. Don't forget to clean under the turning plate—there are almost always little gifts hiding there, too.

11. **Grout:** As in the bathroom, kitchen grout is notoriously difficult to clean. One of my favorite cleaning methods is to put toilet bowl cleaner on the grout lines—the spout of the bottle makes this process easy—then let it sit for ten to fifteen minutes before steaming or wiping clean.

12. **Sink:** This is considered by most scientists to be the dirtiest place in your kitchen. When disinfecting any area, it's important that you spray the cleaner and then allow it to sit for at least thirty seconds before you wipe clean. With

Creating a "Yes" Snack Zone

When our girls are at home, they ask for snacks multiple times throughout the day, which means one of the adults has to say "yes" or "no" and then help the girls get what they are allowed to eat at that time. Recently, however, we created a "yes" snack zone in a kitchen drawer and another "yes" snack zone in the refrigerator. Now they don't have to ask for our permission or help—if it's in one of those two spots, they are welcome to it. Game changer!

These areas are filled with fruits, veggies, string cheese, yogurt, and other healthy options. In the summertime, we store prepackaged granola bars, crackers, dried fruit, pretzels, popcorn, puffs, trail mix, applesauce pouches, and nuts in the trunk of our car. Why? These are snacks that don't melt!

The girls don't currently participate in extracurricular activities during the school year, but during the summertime we're constantly on the go! This is a grab-and-go system that helps us keep the girls fueled and helps us get out the door faster. We don't have to worry about packing snacks before we leave, and we can quickly grab what they need wherever we're going!

the sink, you can sprinkle a bit of baking soda into the bottom and then use a spray bottle to spritz a mixture of vinegar and water. This creates another cool chemical reaction that also helps to fight away lingering germs!

Sharing the Load

Emily and I both enjoy cooking, so we take turns making dinner for the family. After a busy day of teaching, I often find that being alone in the kitchen feels luxurious, especially if I turn on music or a podcast or watch a show on the tablet while I cook. (Noise-canceling headphones are a must!) The actual process of cooking is just one part of mealtime routines. There are lots of different smaller routines that all have to work together to *eventually* make it possible to get dinner on the table.

Making Mealtimes Happen: Routine Breakdown

1. **Meal planning:** Meal planning for the week can involve reading and reviewing recipes, selecting which meals to make and the number of portions, writing out a schedule for which days to serve each recipe, and checking which ingredients you already have.

2. **Grocery shopping:** Grocery shopping includes listing which ingredients you need, making a plan for when to purchase them, and then actually purchasing them. We make small trips to the local grocery store on our block

when walking home from school or work, and then plan a larger grocery run every few weeks. Whatever method you use, it can be helpful to have a plan for the week and to schedule the grocery shopping into your calendar.

3. **Meal prepping:** Meal prepping includes gathering the ingredients you need for a recipe and preparing what can be readied in advance. This typically includes chopping veggies, cooking grains, marinating meat, creating spice mixes, and making sauces/vinaigrettes. You could batch prep tasks once a week or do it before each meal. Either way, it makes it easier and faster when it is time to actually start cooking.

4. **Cooking:** Gather your prepped ingredients and also prepare any remaining ingredients. Remember to reread the recipe and envision the order of events before starting to cook. Then it's time to scoop, pour, stir, mix, or take any other cooking steps! When possible, I'd recommend attempting to wash any prep dishes as you go, to make cleanup easier after the meal.

5. **Preparing the table:** Choose which serving dishes to use and bring them over to the table. Set the table with plates, bowls, utensils, napkins, cups, and whatever else you need for the meal. This is a great part of the routine for kids to learn to help.

6. **Cleaning the table area:** After eating, it's time to move dirty dishes from the table into the kitchen. Encourage

each person to grab what they can carry as they're getting up from the table, to make it a group effort. Then wipe off the table and chairs and sweep the floor.

7. **Daily kitchen cleaning:** It's important to have a daily rhythm for "closing out the kitchen." Tasks could include washing dishes, storing leftover food, wiping counters, sweeping the floor, etc. It's difficult to cook in a space that isn't clean, and it's also *very* easy for bugs and mice to take pleasure in little treats that are left behind. If you don't have a dishwasher, try to have all the prep dishes washed and in the drying rack *before* dinner is served. That way only the serving dishes, plates, and silverware need to be washed afterward.

8. **Weekly kitchen cleaning:** In addition to daily kitchen cleaning, it is also necessary to have a regular rhythm for deep-cleaning the kitchen. This involves tasks like sanitizing the counters, sweeping and mopping the floors, cleaning appliances, and disinfecting the sink. I'd recommend doing a thorough scrub of the kitchen at least once a week.

Over the years we've gradually included our girls in more aspects of our mealtime routines. We want them to learn age-appropriate skills and eventually be able to prepare snacks and meals for themselves independently. Our oldest daughter has graduated from independently cracking eggs to sometimes preparing breakfast for the family. We provide her with the recipe, and she asks for assistance if needed but also adds her own flair. She loves experimenting with food coloring and sprinkles, much to the delight of her younger sisters. Our younger girls don't cook independently yet, but they help to set and clear the table.

I recently shared a breakfast baking experience with Mabel on Instagram, and a woman sent me a DM to say that as a busy working single mom, she assigned each of her two children a night to make dinner. Starting around age eight, they planned and cooked one meal each week. Talk about creative problem-solving and giving your children choice! She said that while one child quickly developed a repertoire of easy, crowd-pleasing recipes—think tacos and pasta—her other child loved experimenting with new recipes. That child later became a chef and at age twenty-six opened her own restaurant. More proof that the home is the perfect, low-stakes training ground for kids to develop real-world skills.

Remember, you don't have to do all the work. You can share responsibilities (like using a meal planning service or trading who cooks/cleans), outsource responsibilities (ordering takeout or scheduling grocery delivery), or eliminate responsibilities (going out for pizza—no cooking or cleaning required!). Those are just a few examples, but consider how you can share the workload for the mealtime routine based on your current rhythms.

INDEPENDENT PRACTICE

Kitchen Gadget Drawer

Does your kitchen gadget drawer jingle every time it opens? If so, it's a clear sign to declutter. Let's approach this practice opportunity with a critical eye and focus on the gadgets you actually use, especially during daily cooking routines.

When you open that gadget drawer, are you met with chaos or can you easily find what you need? While those festive holiday spatulas may bring joy, do you truly need all ten cluttering your prep zone? It's time to trim the fat—pardon the cooking pun—and create a functional kitchen gadget drawer that serves your needs efficiently. Here's a step-by-step approach:

1. **Clear:** Gather all your kitchen gadgets in one area.

2. **Sort:** Categorize the gadgets into categories: Everyday, Special Occasion, Back Stock, What Even *Is* This?

3. **Assess:** Reserve the drawer for everyday gadgets only, focusing on items essential for daily cooking tasks.

4. **Plan:** Contain gadgets in a way that ensures easy accessibility and simple storage after use.

9

A Recipe for Sweet Dreams

Bedrooms often serve multiple purposes, from sleeping to dressing and even functioning as home offices or lounge spaces. The challenge can lie in taming the clutter of clothing and battling the volume of other items that can make your bedroom feel like a storage unit instead of a place for a relaxing retreat.

Nothing can ever quite prepare you for the sleep deprivation of early parenthood. It's a persistent kind of buzz that's always there, always lingering, and that feels like it's never going to go away. As the weeks turn into months, the exhaustion can compound, weighing more heavily with each passing day. My hammer battle with a neighbor in our adjoining building is evidence of the consequences that can arise from a foggy state of mind.

One night, Mabel woke up crying around 3 A.M. As I groggily rolled over in bed, I heard the alarming sound of hammering. I ran into Mabel's room and scooped her up from her crib. Her cries *and* the mysterious pounding stopped. I tried to convince myself that the sound had just been my imagination running wild.

Unfortunately, the following night unfolded in a similar way. In the middle of the night, Mabel started crying and the pounding returned. This time, fueled by a mixture of frustration and determination, I hurled myself out of bed, grabbed my hammer from the toolbox and returned to the nursery. As Mabel sat in her crib, staring at me, I began pounding on the cinder block wall.

"F**k you—get your baby to sleep!" The neighbor's heated words pierced through the thin barrier of the wall.

"She's a baby! Babies cry!" I screamed, my own frustration boiling over as I tightened my grip on the hammer, ready to resume my battle.

"Tyler, *stop!*" Emily said, pulling Mabel from her crib. "Why are you hammering on our wall?"

"F**k you!" the neighbor screamed again.

Now I wanted to cry. I felt like I had hit the first stage of parenthood rock bottom.

The next day, I made a conscious effort to reclaim a sense of clarity amid the chaos. There had to be a solution, a way to navigate through this storm of exhaustion and frustration. And then it struck me—I could simply move the crib to the other side of the room, which was not abutting neighboring apartments.

With heavy hearts we set about rearranging the nursery, sacrificing aesthetics for functionality. We moved the crib to the opposite wall, where Mabel's cries would no longer disturb our neighbor. This would not be the last time we would rearrange furniture in the bedrooms, and looking back, the experience taught us the art of adaptability in our living space.

Simplify Your Sleeping Space

There's a saying: "One's company, two's a crowd, three's a party." Our third child has certainly proven to be a party, and we've now traded the bassinet and toddler bed for a triple bunk bed. That's right—our girls are stacked triple high, and it's made all the difference in their shared bedroom.

With five people sharing two bedrooms, allocating our spaces has been a logistical challenge, and we've had to be intentional about choosing what's stored in each area. Complicating this ever-evolving puzzle has been the sheer lack of closet space in our apartment. One bedroom has built-in closets, but the other one doesn't. For years we made do with hand-me-down furniture and smaller storage pieces. Part of that had to do with being frugal and wanting to use what we already had, and the other part came from lingering questions about whether NYC was going to be our long-term home and if our current apartment would continue to be just enough.

Recently, we chose to invest in a triple wardrobe system for the largest bedroom, providing each girl with a dedicated storage space for folded and hanging clothes, along with upper shelves for out-of-season and "next size" clothing. We now have triple the girls, triple the wardrobes, triple the bunks, triple the fun!

Bedrooms can pose challenges regardless of their size or storage options, because it's easy for them to become clutter traps.

This is what initially made the Great Bedroom Flip so difficult for me. There's also a good chance you might be sleeping *on top of* some of that clutter. Decluttering common bedroom clutter traps (try saying that five times fast) can help your bedroom go from feeling like a storage unit to a relaxing retreat.

Declutter *This:* Bedroom Clutter Traps

1. **Nightstands:** The purpose of a nightstand is to give you access to the *most* important things that you need before you go to sleep or when you wake up in the morning. A current book, glasses, charger, a bottle of water—what else do you need? If you're storing sentimental items, cards, important papers, books that you've already read, extra pairs of eyeglasses (the list could go on), it's time to edit!

2. **Under the bed:** A king-sized bed is traditionally seventy-six inches wide by eighty inches long, and most mattresses are twelve to fourteen inches off the ground. We're sleeping on top of prime organizational real estate! This large, flat, "out of sight, out of mind" area might seem like the perfect place to store out-of-season clothing, extra bedding, books, papers, etc. But be careful not to make this the spot where items go to die. Personally, I don't want to sleep on top of a haphazard pile of random clutter, so finding alternative storage solutions is essential.

3. **Top of closets:** Closets are a precious resource, yet the very top shelves can be organizationally tricky. This area isn't easily accessible, but it can be a good storage location for

items that you know you want to keep but don't need to access regularly. It could be a place to keep out-of-season clothing, luggage, important papers, sentimental items, and extra bedding, or a spot to hide gifts.

4. **Dresser drawers:** Are you the type of person who matches their underwear to their outfit? According to an unscientific study, the majority of people do, and it may be TMI, but I'm one of them. I have a capsule wardrobe with four core colors—navy, burgundy, olive, and tan. I checked the back of my dresser drawers and found a stack of black underwear that I *never* wear. Why would I—they don't match my outfits. After sharing this fact with Emily, she checked the back of her dresser drawers and discovered several nursing bras that she still had stored, even though our youngest stopped breastfeeding years ago. Dresser drawers are clutter traps!

5. **Flat surfaces:** The top of dressers and nightstands are often convenient "drop zones," and can easily become littered with receipts, keys, books, papers, and *more*. I'm not sure who first said this, but I've heard people argue, "Better on a table than on the floor." As things can quickly start to pile up on table surfaces, leading to a disorganized mess, I'm not convinced that's sound advice.

I generally strive to keep things tidy, but I have a confession: Visual clutter really bothers me, and if I'm in a rush and don't have time to fully deal with things, I'll just stash them in furniture with doors or drawers, or toss them in a basket, so I don't have to look at the mess. Emily prefers to leave things out as a visual reminder that they need to be properly dealt with, rather than letting clutter accumulate out of sight. My chosen approach leads to bins and baskets filling up with a random assortment of left-out treasures, causing "Where's my ____?" moments from Emily and the girls. They'll go to exactly the spot where they left something, wondering where it could have gone, and then discover it days later in one of my clutter baskets. I'm aware this is a problem, and I'm working on it.

One of the things that has helped is to opt for furniture pieces without easily accessible storage compartments like cabinets and drawers where I'll be tempted to hide items away. A few years ago, I designed and built myself a bedside table out of a suitcase I'd purchased at an auction with my grandma. The legs of the table were a "trash to treasure" discovery, and my makeshift table provided a flat surface next to the bed for a cup of water and books. I put two baskets on the floor underneath the table for my slippers and magazines. My side of the bed looks beautifully minimal and crafty, and there is no place to accumulate clutter or stash it away indefinitely. Emily has a small ottoman next to her side of the bed and it serves a similar purpose. The top of the ottoman has a flat surface, and the lid can be lifted off to reveal a shallow area for storing her phone charger and a book.

Decluttering with Kids

As adults, we are ultimately in control of the items that come in and out of our homes and the ways those items are stored. We're the ones who carry the majority of things in from the car. We're the ones who dictate how money is spent, and what behaviors around shopping look like. When it comes to items that are often stored in children's bedrooms, we are in charge of setting boundaries around the volume of stuffed animals, books, hand-me-down clothing, pieces of sentimental artwork, dress-up-clothes, and toys. But that doesn't mean we shouldn't sometimes consult our kids and take their opinions into consideration.

Having a shared language and system for decluttering is important.

The mistake many parents make is that they start the decluttering process and too often toss or donate things that don't look "valuable" to us but that might have real sentimental value to our kids. Imagine if someone decided for you that your box of childhood photos was too full and put it to you this way: "You need to get rid of half of the photos, and if you can't make the decisions yourself, then I'm going to make the decisions for you." This is, in effect, what we sometimes do to our kids.

Stuffed animals, baby dolls, artwork, and even small scraps of paper—at one time or another these were all deemed "highly sentimental" by our girls. These were not the items through which to start teaching lessons on decluttering. However, there are several *other* items that are often stored in the bedroom that can be the perfect starting place for embracing decluttering with your kids.

For starters, kids need to see that decluttering is a regular family rhythm. Physically and developmentally, kids are constantly growing, so it's reasonable to assume that you'll be getting bigger or newer versions of things as they grow. In some ways, that makes the four steps of decluttering fairly obvious. Clear, sort, assess, and plan are four processes that kids can learn to understand. Here's what this could look like, with an emotionally low-stakes item that all kids need, wear, and eventually outgrow: pajamas.

1. **Clear:** "I've noticed your pajama drawer is looking a bit full, and you've gotten so much taller since the last time we got you new ones. It's probably time to clear out your drawer so that we can see what still fits." (Empty drawer together.)

2. **Sort:** Work together to sort pajamas into what fits and what is too small. Try on as needed. Take time to ask about which ones are their favorites: consider colors, styles, fabric, etc.

3. **Assess:** Determine which pajamas to keep, which ones to donate, and which ones to store in a hand-me-down bin for siblings/cousins/friends/neighbors. It can be helpful for

kids to see this process of giving items that they have outgrown to another kid who can actually use them.

4. **Plan:** Fold up the kids' pajamas that still fit and put them back into the drawer, while determining if they need any additional pajamas for the next size/season.

Having a shared language and system for decluttering is important. As your kids become more comfortable with decluttering, you can eventually progress to more complicated categories of items. Emily recently guided the girls through the decluttering steps in their playroom, and they were able to quickly identify their favorite baby dolls (ones with eyes that open and shut, that have open mouths for bottles and pacifiers and play food, and that could have their clothes changed—the more realistic the better!). They were willing to bag up the unwanted dolls, Emily listed them for free on our local Buy Nothing group, and a preschool teacher happily picked them up for her classroom, where they will continue to be played with and loved. The goal here is to equip your child with decision-making skills that last a lifetime. Introducing decluttering as a normal and predictable part of life early on is key. A decluttering calendar can help!

Bedroom Zoning

As I've explained, we're constantly negotiating over the shared spaces in our apartment and have to intentionally think about how we allocate real estate. The same is true with our bedrooms.

Establishing clear zones in a bedroom can help you to make organizational decisions.

Bedroom Zones

1. **Sleeping:** Whether your room features a twin-, full-, queen-, or king-sized bed, creating space for rest is essential. The sleeping zone typically takes up the most square footage in a bedroom, and from bed frame to mattress to bedding, it's important to choose items that promote comfort and relaxation. It's also important to have some sort of nightstand or table for organizing things like books, chargers, sound machines, sleep masks, or earplugs. Also consider where to store an additional set of bedding so you can always have a fresh set of sheets accessible.

2. **Getting ready:** Whether you have a tiny closet like mine or an expansive walk-in closet, optimizing organization in the space you have is key. Consider organizing items by category or arranging them by color to enhance efficiency. Design systems based on how you naturally get dressed and ready for the day.

3. **Relaxation/self-care:** Although relaxation and self-care can sometimes feel elusive, this is the room in which to prioritize creating a dedicated space for activities that bring you joy. You can use bins, baskets, or available furniture surfaces to create a place for your favorite

relaxation item, whether it's a book, crossword puzzle, streaming device, or candle and lotion.

4. **Sentimental/important files:** It's important to have a designated space to store sentimental papers and crucial documents, like insurance records, medical papers, birth certificates, passports, etc. In our apartment, that place is in our bedroom. Consider investing in a fireproof safe to securely store those items.

5. **Work from home:** Bedrooms are typically separated from common areas in a home, meaning they're private and quiet, which can make the room ideal for work. If you are tight on space, get creative! Emily has a dresser in her closet that has a pull-out desk feature between the drawers, which easily converts the dresser into a desk and is neatly stowed away when not in use.

Choice Within Boundaries

In their wardrobes, each of our three girls has their own special "joy shelf" at standing height, where they proudly display their most treasured trinkets and cherished sentimental items. Each has a jewelry box and several small clear containers for organization. Their joy shelves are strictly off-limits for Emily and me, allowing them full autonomy to arrange items as they please. This is an example of "choice within boundaries." As parents, we've set the boundary on where small treasures are stored, and the girls have the freedom to choose what to keep and how to display their special items. It's been a way to offer our girls opportunities for decision-making in low-pressure situations. Since much of our apartment and their bedroom is considered "shared space," it's been fun to see each of them carve out a personalized area that reflects their individuality and uniqueness, and it offers them a valuable chance to practice determining what holds significance to them. I think everyone needs their own special "joy shelf"!

Bedroom Bliss

"Why do the kids here have to sleep in bedrooms all alone at night? Don't they get scared?" Matilda asked us after visiting her cousins' new house in Indiana. Until recently her cousins had shared a bedroom in the apartment directly below ours, but in the land of suburbia, separate kid bedrooms are the norm. The concept baffled our girls.

In New York City and in many other areas around the world, kids sharing bedrooms *is* the norm, but it comes with its own set of challenges and can require careful negotiation. Sometimes busy parents reach out to me to schedule a "Tidy Tips call with Tidy Dad"—doesn't that have a nice ring to it?—seeking advice on how to optimize their spaces, especially with kids.

"I'm really struggling to create individual spaces for my kids in their shared bedroom," Rebecca told me. She had scheduled a call to discuss the post-decluttering reality she was entering into with her family. They lived in a two-bedroom condo in New Jersey and had recently given their six-year-old daughter and five-year-old son the larger bedroom to share. (I guess our family has become somewhat of a trendsetter in encouraging parents in two-bedroom spaces to share the smaller bedroom and give the kids the larger one.)

For Rebecca, decluttering had been the easy part, but the bedroom's long, narrow layout, with a large, shared closet at one end and an expansive window at the other, presented a design dilemma. Besides a queen-sized bed, a wardrobe, and a tall bookcase, the room lacked additional furniture. Rebecca was struggling to decide what else to bring into the room and how to arrange the space to meet her children's current needs, while also trying to anticipate their future needs so that it could be a place that continued to work for them long-term.

Prioritizing the allocation of space is a crucial first step when designing shared areas. I advised Rebecca to name what wasn't working, identify the specific zones she wanted to establish, and envision how she wanted her children to be able to utilize the space.

> ### What We Kept
>
> You don't need to keep *all* the baby clothes as a memento—in fact, we saved just one item! We have one tiny onesie that we framed and hung on a wall in the girls' bedroom. We photographed all three girls wearing it when they were newborns. We don't need *all* the cute onesies the girls once wore, but this one represents that entire infant era!

"Right now the room feels sparse, and while there's open space to play, it's just not working for them," Rebecca said. "I want them to feel like they have their own areas, and also have space to play together. I'd really love to create two separate sleeping zones, possibly with bunk beds or loft beds, maybe a reading and play zone near the window, and also a place for the kids to complete their homework, make their arts and crafts creations, and build LEGOs. I also need some ideas about how to organize all their things."

Having a clear vision for the intended use of a space is essential for creating an effective organizational plan. Here are some of our favorite organizational ideas that can be effective for both kids' and adults' bedrooms.

Bedroom Organization Ideas

1. **Bed caddies:** Bed caddies can be Velcroed directly onto the side or foot of bed frames and provide easily accessible storage. This is especially helpful for bunk beds because kids on the top bunk can't reach a nightstand.

2. **Over-the-door organizer:** Adding baskets, shelves, or mesh pockets to the back of a door can help keep collections of small objects organized. They could be used to organize stuffed animals, dolls, or dress-up accessories, or they could contain items like socks, shoes, neckties, belts, jewelry, or scarves.

3. **Bookcases:** Bookcases help organize the obvious, but they also provide flat surfaces ideal for smaller organization pieces like jewelry boxes, trays, or bins.

4. **Baskets and bins:** Large floor baskets in a bedroom can be used for throw blankets, pillows, or even "half-dirty" clothes that aren't ready for the laundry hamper yet, but

that you don't want to put back into your closet. In a kid's room, they can help to corral categories of toys like dolls, cars, or trains.

5. **Zippered storage bins:** Zippered storage bins or vacuum seal bags can be effective for keeping extra clothing organized and protected from damage. They can also work well for storing extra linens and blankets.

6. **File box for sentimental papers:** Designating a storage location for sentimental papers helps to keep them contained and organized. Our girls each have their own file box with separate folders for toddlerhood through twelfth grade, setting clear, organized boundaries for how much to keep.

7. **Clip-on book lights:** Reading books in the evening is a daily family rhythm for us. At the end of a busy day, we tuck all three girls into bed at the same time, and let them read until they fall asleep. They each have their own clip-on book light that allows them to look at books with the overhead light off. The lights are rechargeable using a USB cable, eliminating the need for batteries and making them perfect for travel activities, such as car rides.

8. **Charging station:** Our girls love their audio players, and we keep them charged using a central charging station on a shelf on their bookcase. This command center serves as a

one-stop place to charge devices and wireless headphones, and it keeps cords neatly organized.

9. **Zippered bedding:** We replaced the duvet, duvet insert, and sheet sets on each bunk layer with zippered bedding. It's made all the difference! The bedding set goes on like a fitted sheet, with a bottom sheet sewn into the elastic panel and a top blanket featuring zippers. This keeps each bunk neat and simplifies the process of washing and changing bedding.

10. **Wall hooks:** There's always *something* to hang in the bedroom—pajamas, robes, coats, bags, headphones, etc. Just like the back of doors, walls can offer additional organizational space if you choose to use them. Consider where you could strategically install a set of hooks in each bedroom for flexible and convenient organization.

Dust Bunnies Beware

I enjoy cleaning in the early weekday mornings, but bedroom cleaning day is the trickiest to get finished before school. On Instagram, I like to announce, "It's bedroom cleaning day, but you can't clean bedrooms while people are asleep. I've tried." That joke lands every time.

But it's no joke that bedrooms are notorious for accumulating mess, dust, and other *signs of life*. Cleaning the bedroom isn't just about changing sheets. I'm choosing my words very carefully here; suffice it to say there are so many dirty things about our bedrooms. I've cleaned bedrooms not only in our apartment, but also after countless rental stays at our cottage. I've stumbled upon things like dog food bags, an assortment of fake eyelashes, half-used bottles of perfume, and an abandoned bowl of cereal with rotten milk. The lingering combination of those scents nearly knocked me out!

After tackling those messes, I consider myself to be somewhat of an expert on this topic, so I recommend following these tips to deal with the *dirtiest* of bedroom issues. Here's a look at the Bedroom Dirty Dozen:

Bedroom Dirty Dozen

1. **Under the bed:** This area can be a clutter and dust trap! If you need the organization space, consider large storage containers that are easy to slide in and out. Keeping it clear makes cleaning easier, and if you have a robot vacuum, it can just roll right underneath, clean, and roll back out.

2. **Bed frames:** Bed frames dominate bedroom space and have numerous connected parts, like headboard, rails, and slats (and a ladder, if it's a bunk bed). These parts tend to collect dust, but can be easily cleaned and sanitized with a damp cloth. While you're wiping the bed frame, don't forget to also look down and clean those baseboards.

3. **Inside wardrobes/closets:** The amount of dust that accumulates in the corners of closets and wardrobes can be shocking. Even though items are contained behind closed doors, it's still crucial to maintain cleanliness in this space. Every few months, remove items from shelves and drawers for a thorough wipe-down to ensure a clean storage space. This is also a great opportunity to declutter.

4. **Door handles:** Every room has them, and in every room they're probably dirty! While cleaning door handles, go ahead and wipe down the front and back of doors and their frames. Don't overlook the top of the doorframe, as it tends to attract dust.

5. **Curtains:** Curtains and window shades are dust magnets. Before washing, check the tag for cleaning instructions. Additionally, if your windows are drafty or noisy, consider investing in insulated curtains. Blackout shades with light-gap blockers are also great options for bedrooms.

6. **Pillows:** Here's a reminder to replace your pillows at a minimum of every two years, although the lifespan can vary based on the material. Pillows made of foam may last longer, while down or down-alternative pillows may need replacing after only one year. Most pillows are machine-washable and can be washed on a cool setting with mild detergent, then tumbled dry on low heat.

7. **Bedding:** Bedding also has varying lifespans, with sheets typically lasting longer than pillows. Sheets, pillowcases, comforters, duvet inserts, and duvet covers each have different washing frequency recommendations. If you notice stains, cold water and dish soap can often effectively remove them!

8. **Mattresses:** Vacuum your mattress regularly to remove dust and debris, and don't forget the sides and seams. To remove stains, use a mild detergent with warm water, but avoid soaking the mattress to prevent mold growth. To freshen the mattress, sprinkle baking soda, let it sit, then vacuum. I highly recommend using a zippered mattress encasement (with a Velcro seal) to protect your mattress against bedbugs, spills, dust, bacteria, and bodily fluids and to help prolong its lifespan.

9. **Comforters:** There are two types of comforters: those with duvet covers and those without. Comforters with duvet covers require less frequent washing, since it's the cover that makes contact with skin, not the comforter itself. Duvet covers are similar to sheets, so whether or not you use a top sheet influences how often you should wash the cover.

10. **Houseplants:** To keep your houseplants healthy, it's essential to clean them regularly. Dust can accumulate on their leaves, hindering their growth. Give them a gentle wipe with a damp rag or sponge to maintain their vitality. Your plants will appreciate it!

11. **Jewelry and accessory storage:** Jewelry boxes, trays, and holders can harbor dirt, oils, and bacteria from daily wear. Items like earrings, rings, and watches can accumulate grime over time, especially if not cleaned or sanitized regularly. Make sure you don't neglect this category!

12. **Laundry hampers:** Laundry hampers can harbor bacteria from our dirty clothes. If your hamper is fabric, you can probably clean it in the washing machine. For other materials, wipe them down regularly or spray them with disinfectant cleaner. If you clean with bleach, make sure to rinse the surface thoroughly with water to remove any remaining bleach residue before refilling with clothes.

INDEPENDENT PRACTICE

Getting Intimate with a Socks and Underwear Refresh

When it comes to underwear, there's the age-old question of "boxers or briefs?" The more important question might be, "When was the last time you gave your drawers a refresh?" Did you know that experts recommend that you replace your underwear every six to twelve months, depending upon the number of pairs that you have? If that frequency comes as a shock, it's probably time to get some new skivvies. While you're at it, go ahead and look at your socks, too.

1. **Clear:** Empty your sock and underwear drawers.

2. **Sort:** Categorize items by underwear type and sock type.

3. **Assess:** Examine underwear/socks for fit, condition, comfort, and holes!

4. **Plan:** Fold or roll underwear/socks and return them to the drawer. Order more as needed.

10

Making the Glam Room Sparkle

Bathrooms are the site of very strategic and vital work. It's important to organize the space so that it works for you and not against you. Regardless of how many people share your bathroom, you deserve to have a glam room that sparkles!

There's one room in our apartment that *really* gets people talking. I'm talking about the glam room, aka the bathroom. Ratios and proportional relationships are an important part of my teaching vocabulary, and it's that ever-present ratio for our life in New York City that's the subject of all those messages:

😀😊😊😊😊 : 🚽

Yes, that's one man, one woman, and three girls all sharing one toilet. In this modern age, our family of five shares one small bathroom. Our bathroom includes a toilet, a sink with a medicine cabinet over it, and a mini bathtub—only little Margaret can still comfortably lie down in the bathtub. The standing area measures two feet by three feet. There is not a linen closet, or any bathroom drawers. (Drawers are an endangered species in our apartment.)

People ask me all the time how we manage, and they often wonder out loud what will happen when our girls become teenagers. Others think that our bathroom's location right off the kitchen is unsanitary and probably smelly. To them I cheekily say, "I'll be sure to file your complaint with the architect who designed our apartment in 1914. But just so you know, they don't frequently check their email." As for what we'll do with three teenagers? The bathroom might be the least of our problems! We'll see—that will be a different season of our lives, and at the moment it's still about a decade away.

The organizational real estate in our bathroom is incredibly valuable, and it's important for us to allocate that space based on our current needs and rhythms of life. This is one room where it has been especially important to ditch the *hypothetical someday* and consider what's needed *right now.* Right now we need a step stool so Margaret can reach the counter. Right now we need a toilet seat that has a smaller seat built into the lid for the small bottoms that sit on it. We're not thinking about teenagers, because we don't have any who live with us!

Flush Out the Chaos

Whether you have one bathroom for five people or five and a half bathrooms for four people—I'm referring to my younger sister's spacious farmhouse in Kentucky—it's important to organize the space so that it works for you and not against you. After all, bathrooms are a hub of very specific and *important* work.

To bring order to any space, you first have to make sense of the mess. To start, stand back and take a good look at the logistics of your bathroom. Open every cabinet, every drawer, any closets, pull back the shower curtain, and take a long look at the volume of items that you're dealing with. Then it's time to apply the decluttering steps: clear, sort, assess, and plan!

You can't make your glam room sparkle if there is a high volume of stuff crowding the space. Here's a list of predictable bathroom items that are easy to accumulate and easy to forget about . . . until they fall on your head when you open the medicine cabinet.

Declutter *This:* Bathroom Edition

1. **Bathroom towels/washcloths:** How many towels are too many? If you have enough for everyone you live with to use a different towel each day of the week, it might be time to pare down your selection. Consider things like how many people live in your home, how many people you typically host overnight at a time in your space, and how often you do laundry. Also check the quality of the towels and washcloths you're currently using (any holes or stains?), because items that are used and washed frequently don't last forever! If you have towels you're ready to get rid of, you can donate them to your local animal shelter or pet shops.

2. **Hair accessories:** I'm the hair braider in our home. French braids are my current specialty, so we have an array of water spray bottles, detanglers, clips, scrunchies, and elastic hair bands on hand. The girls have a choice in the accessories they want to keep, but we've set a physical boundary limit by storing them all in one designated caddy. As you declutter, look for any hair accessories that are worn out, have lost their elasticity, or tangle or pull hair.

3. **Nail polish:** I don't wear nail polish, but I live with three little ones who are obsessed with colorful nails. As you declutter, you should open each nail polish bottle, inspect the brush, check if there are any particles floating around in the bottle, and see if the polish is dried out or a gooey thick texture. It's a clear sign that the nail polish is past its prime!

4. **Toiletries you never use:** If you don't *like* it, then you probably won't *use* it! Let it go! Who cares if it was a free sample or something left over from a hotel bathroom? Keep what you actually *enjoy* using!

I don't expect you to drop this book and begin decluttering your bathroom right away, but when you do, channel me, Tidy Dad, and ask yourself these questions:

Did you find any excess toiletries, shampoos, perfumes, cosmetics, nail polish, soaps, or facial creams? Do you really need ten tubes of toothpaste or a half dozen bottles of shampoo?

Even if you have the space to store all those extras, is that really the best use of it?

Does it look like you are planning for a doomsday scenario?

On our own decluttering journey, we've discovered that it's important to have that inner dialogue. Ask yourself questions, and probe deeper. Decluttering is the time to scrutinize what you have and why you have it. When it comes to the bathroom, the goal is efficiency and practicality. We no longer allocate space in our apartment for doomsday scenarios. We tried that during the pandemic, but quickly ran out of places to stash the toilet paper.

No matter the room or space you're working on, every decluttering session invites you to learn something about yourself.

Not all toiletries and cosmetics are created equal, of course, and it's important to interrogate the *why* when you are selecting items to keep. If you love the smell of a product or the way it makes you feel (even if you use it very occasionally), then maybe you should keep it. But if it doesn't fit your quality control standards, and you realize you never or rarely use it, then why is it taking up valuable space in your bathroom? Personally, I've ditched most men's grooming products with any strong scents, because they give me a headache and they remind me of my chaperone duties at middle school dances. *Oof.*

While you are acting as the quality control inspector, also check the expiration dates on products. I learned my lesson big-time one morning when I'd run out of face lotion and decided to use one I found in the back of the cabinet. It was expired, but I decided to ignore that, and lathered it on my face. Within two minutes, my face turned bright red and became blotchy. Lesson learned. If it's expired, it's time for it to go!

No matter the room or space you're working on, every declut-tering session invites you to learn something about yourself. The bathroom is one area of the home I recommend decluttering at least quarterly. It's easy to overbuy items when you can't quickly locate exactly what you need. The goal is to reduce the volume, while simultaneously securing more space to efficiently organize the items that are actually essential and have qualities that en-hance your life. Those are the items that should be easily acces-sible!

Zone Your Way to Organizational Bliss

More than any other room in the home, the bathroom must be a clean and functional space. Whether your entire family shares one bathroom or you have more bathrooms than people, bath-rooms are usually *the place* for routines, especially in the morning and evening.

One of the many fabulous features of our tiny apartment bathroom is that I can stand directly in front of our medicine cabinet, stretch out my arms in any direction, and reach any toiletry or cosmetic item that I could possibly need. Talk about efficiency, right? (Sometimes I think I should be a real estate agent—I have the gift of spin.)

Remember, the goal of zoning is to organize items into areas based on how, when, and where you use them, so that you can easily access them in the right location. Regardless of square footage, establishing zones that work in support of your routines can help you maximize space and easily access the items you need.

Bathroom Zones

1. **Getting clean:** Your getting clean zone consists of the shower or tub area and the storage or organization areas nearby. We have a tub with limited ledges for bath and shower products, so we use a rolling cart directly next to the tub to organize those things. If you have little ones, you may also want to carve out some space for bath toys.

2. **Daily prep:** Daily prep consists of brushing your teeth, washing your face, applying makeup, and brushing and styling your hair, so it makes sense that things associated with these grooming routines should live near the vanity, sink, or part of the bathroom where you have access to a mirror. This is *not* the area of the bathroom to store back stock. In this zone, it's important to have what you need, when you need it.

3. **Special maintenance:** Sometimes you'll have occasion for a little extra zhuzhing up, perhaps with nail polish, glitter

makeup, or unicorn headbands. If you're not a little girl, perhaps it's a hair trimmer (every man in your life should have one of these), nail clippers, tweezers, or a magnified mirror. These are not everyday items, and so it's not necessary for them to be within immediate reach, but they still need a place of their own.

4. **Back stock:** Back stock includes things like extra toiletries, toilet paper, and supplies for caring for young children. They need an organizational home, yet shouldn't take up prime real estate. Baskets, bins, and shelves can be helpful for organizing these items in bathroom cabinets or a nearby closet. With back stock, make sure to set clear boundaries around the volume of items to store.

5. **Bathroom maintenance:** Bathrooms see a lot of action, and it's important to store and organize the necessary cleaners and products to keep the glam room sparkling. If you have little ones, store cleaning products out of their reach (or put kid locks on low cabinets). Also, always make sure a clean plunger is easily accessible!

A few years ago, our apartment was photographed for an article in *Better Homes & Gardens* magazine, and the bathroom took center stage. Most of the bathrooms in magazines these days feel as if they're the same square footage as our entire apartment, so our little bathroom standing up for the tiny bathrooms of the world felt especially nice. The writer of the article spent three days in our apartment, including one whole day of staging, followed by two days with the photographer.

The resulting photos were beautiful. They were able to mask the mismatched tile, the spray foam insulation to keep the bugs and mice out, and the vanity doors that don't quite close shut. The room has not looked quite as beautiful since! It was a bit like putting lipstick on a pig.

Whenever I want to reminisce about our bathroom's day of ultimate beauty, I can just grab that magazine and look at the photos during *reading time.* By the way, that's my one subtle nod to potty humor. You can't write a bathroom chapter without at least one subtle potty joke.

What isn't a joke was that as part of the prep for the shoot, we got to select some new bathroom organization pieces for the magazine to feature. Many of the items we'd previously used were a hodgepodge of bins we'd repurposed for various supplies over the years. When choosing new items, we actually took the time to measure, and selected pieces that fit the space really well.

The new items supported many of the organizational hacks I spoke about to *Better Homes & Gardens.* Here are some of those hacks:

Bathroom Organization Products

- **Three-tier carts:** These carts are an easy way to add vertical levels of storage to your bathroom, and are versatile for any room in the home. A cart in your "Getting clean" or "Daily prep" zones can add additional toiletry storage. On each level you can add smaller bins and containers to partition the levels into functional multileveled storage.

- **One-sided rolling carts:** We have two carts on either side of our vanity. One fits into the little gap between our vanity and toilet, and the other slides between our vanity and tub. They are only five inches wide and are able to face either to the left or right, depending on whether you want the shelves to be open or closed to the room. These carts can help provide additional storage for the "Bathroom maintenance" or "Getting clean" zones. If you have a small bathroom, this can help you maximize every square inch of real estate.

- **Storage benches:** Flat surfaces in bathrooms are handy for towels, clothes, or even to sit on as you are dressing or undressing. A storage bench with built-in shelves can add multiple levels of storage without taking up additional space. We can't fit one in our apartment bathroom, but in our cottage bathroom we have a storage bench that can fit eight folded towels, and that also provides a flat surface for toiletry bags and other bathroom items.

- **Hooks:** I wish I could just wave my magic wand and remove the towel bars from all bathrooms and replace them with multiple hooks instead. I also like adding hooks that clip on to the shower curtain rod or any remaining towel bars. These are super handy for hanging washcloths, articles of clothing that need to dry, or damp swimsuits.

- **Baskets and bins:** In the bathroom, clear plastic or acrylic bins work incredibly well, because you can see what is inside and they are also easy to wipe clean. We added bins to the inside of our medicine cabinet to hold small toiletries, toothbrushes, and cosmetics.

- **Stackable drawers:** It's time to ditch stackable bins with lids and invest in stackable drawers. They work well under sinks or in cabinets, and are easier to access because you can slide out one at a time without the entire stack tumbling over (I'm speaking from experience!).

- **Over-the-toilet storage:** The vertical space over the toilet can be a useful place to put shelving or a cabinet. This can be a great place to add baskets and bins to store toiletry back stock or artfully display toilet paper. Pro tip: Extra toilet paper should *always* be easily accessible.

Pro Tip

Don't start shopping for organizers or storage until you've decluttered, sketched out your zones, and carefully measured your space. It's like creating a blueprint, but for organization. This level of attention and detail is a bit like playing a game of Tetris, and it's so satisfying when the right pieces come together to maximize every square inch.

If you want to achieve that magazine-quality level of organization, you have to start by precisely measuring the space so that you can select the *just right* organizational product. Inches, centimeters, and sometimes millimeters can make all the difference if you want to have a really functional, organized bathroom. The stackable drawers we added to the inside of our vanity cabinet have transformed our daily prep zones. We each have a drawer, and it contains all the small items that help elevate us into the walking supermodels that we are. Beauty takes time, so we can't waste that time trying to locate what we need!

Making Things Routine

Life happens, messes happen, and it's necessary to spend time scrubbing away the dirt, grime, and fingerprints that have been left behind. In our bathroom, we're always battling things like toothpaste buildup and clogged drains (remember, our building was built in 1914), but they're no match for this Tidy Dad. I even taught myself how to take apart the bathroom drain stopper and put it back together to keep that water flowing.

Bathroom Dirty Dozen

1. **Plugs:** Push-and-pull, pop-up, lift-and-turn, flip-it, toe-touch, trip lever. These sound like dance moves, but they are the six most common types of plugs in a bathroom. If you're having trouble with a tub, sink, or toilet filling or draining properly, chances are there's an issue with the plug. A thorough cleaning can often fix the issue!

2. **Drains:** Drains are the gateway to pipes and consist of several connected parts. As gross as it sounds, it's very easy for dirt, skin flakes, and hair to bind to soap scum on the walls of drainpipes, which can cause clogs. Running very

hot water through the drain can often do the trick to help clear them, but sometimes you'll need a bottled declogger or snake hair clog remover.

3. **Filters:** Filters allow water to flow through faucets and other appliances like your dishwasher and washing machine and help trap unwanted particles. Their job is to stop gunk from getting through, and they can become clogged over time. The good news is that most filters are typically easy to remove and clean with hot water! The tricky part can be finding them, so it can be helpful to go on a little scavenger hunt and make a list of *all* the filters in your home, and then make a plan for regularly checking them. I recommend once a quarter.

4. **Toilet seat rims:** The toilet bowl brush is typically used to clean the insides of the toilet bowl, but it's also important to use that brush to scrub the part of the rim where the water flows downward into the bowl. This area of the toilet is functionally important, as it allows water to flow into the basin to push all the unmentionables down into the base of the toilet. Make sure it's clean!

5. **Toilet seat bumpers and screws:** The bumpers provide a gap between the toilet seat and rim, and the screws keep the toilet seat affixed to the bowl. When either of these are loose, the toilet seat can be a bit wobbly. The bumpers and screws are also both traps for germs and dirty stains. Don't neglect this part of the toilet when cleaning.

6. **Shower heads:** In addition to delivering water to your soaped-up scalp, your shower head is effectively a large filter. Like the filters in your sink, it can become clogged over time due to dirt or hard-water buildup. Shower heads have parts that are removable, and cleaning them with a brush and soap can bring them back to pristine condition. If your shower head is leaking, there are special products on the market to tighten the seal.

7. **Baseboards:** Baseboards are dirt and dust magnets but are easy to clean with a microfiber cloth and water or with any multisurface cleaner. Once they're clean, you can repel dirt and dust from your baseboards by wiping them with a dryer sheet. A word of caution: Once you start cleaning your bathroom baseboards, you may no longer be able to use any bathroom—whether a friend's or a public restroom—without looking down to check.

8. **Light fixtures:** These are also dust magnets! When the light fixture and bulbs are cool, you can unscrew the parts and run the fixture under warm water and then wipe it clean. Don't put the light bulb in the water, but you can dust it with a dry cloth. Afterward, your glam room will truly sparkle!

9. **Air vents:** The bathroom air vent, if you're lucky enough to have one, helps to suck air out of the room and transfer it to the outside. You can use the stick attachment on a vacuum to clean the outside of the air vent, or you can

unscrew it from the ceiling to clean the inside and outside. If your vent has a built-in light, see "Light fixtures," above!

10. **Shower curtains:** Whether they're fabric or plastic, you can wash your shower curtain and shower curtain liner. It's helpful to wash these items on a gentle cycle, using your choice of laundry detergent. Once it's clean, rehang it in the bathroom and then allow it to air-dry.

11. **Bath toys:** As much fun as they are, bath toys are notorious water and mold traps. Once infested with mold, plastic toys can be incredibly difficult to clean. Here's my rubber ducky strategy—plug the bottom hole with hot glue. You lose the squirting feature, but this creates a tight seal, preventing water from getting inside!

12. **Grout:** This might be the worst of the bunch. Grout is notoriously difficult to clean, but there are a few tools that can help: a pressurized steam cleaner, an abrasive sponge, or a small brush (like an extra toothbrush). See page 173 for my grout-cleaning strategy using toilet bowl cleaner. You can also create a paste with baking soda, warm water, and dish soap. Pour white vinegar along the grout lines first, and then smear the paste on and scrub. It can work wonders!

Guest Prep

Let's talk about how to prepare for other people using your bathroom, including people who pry, shall we? Here are the top four places to check or clean in preparation for hosting guests in your home!

1. **Sink:** Wipe down the sink, the faucet, and the front of the cabinet or vanity. Lay out a clean hand towel and make sure that the soap dispenser is filled—you don't want anyone walking out of your bathroom with grubby paws.

2. **Toilet:** Clean the outside of the toilet, including the sides, base, seat, and bowl.

3. **Floor:** Give the floor a good sweep, wipe off those baseboards, and empty the trash.

4. **Drawers/cabinets:** Don't waste your time reorganizing anything here. Just add a Post-it note that says, "Stop Snooping."

The Great Morning Shuffle

In our apartment, we're five people sharing a small space, and in the morning, all those people are sharing an incredibly small bathroom. Sometimes it feels like our bathroom is a clown car with more and more people squeezing in and spilling out. There are times when privacy and discretion are important, but it seems like when "the Great Morning Shuffle" is underway, privacy goes out the window. One girl is using the potty. One is brushing her hair. The other is running in and out of the bathroom trying to get her baby dolls ready. I have an on-time school drop-off streak going at the moment, but all five of us navigating the bathroom at the same time was a pain point at the start of the school year. We had to figure out a system to stagger bathroom use.

We typically have an hour between breakfast and getting out the door. It should feel like we have *plenty of time,* but sometimes it feels like we're herding cats. The girls can't be trusted to eat breakfast in their school clothes, so once the breakfast dishes are cleared, their morning task sequence commences. Once teeth are brushed, shoes are on, and the girls are standing by the door, that's when I get dressed—my capsule wardrobe really comes in handy—and make myself presentable for my students. If I'm dressed for school any earlier, it's like I become a sticky-hands magnet!

We recently started using a morning checklist for each girl. Their checklists are posted on the refrigerator so that they are visible to all of us, and the checklists have helped to reduce the number of beautifully positive, encouraging, and motivational verbal reminders Emily and I have to give them. We purchased reusable checklists that allow us to record the list of tasks, and then there's a fun little "X" or "✓" tab that the girls can toggle back and forth, showing whether a task has been completed.

Here are the items on each checklist: eat breakfast, put pajamas away, get dressed, make bed, brush teeth, brush hair, pack snack, pack water, put socks on.

On Margaret's checklist we wrote the word representing the task *and* included a picture. This is a helpful strategy, because she can't read yet. The best part of having this chart is that Emily and I don't have to remind the girls of what to do next. When I ask them if they've done something, they enjoy saying, "Dad, just check my list!" That's attitude that I'm okay with.

INDEPENDENT PRACTICE

Set Up Your Glam Station

You deserve your own personal glam station. We all need one! Consider which items are most important for your routine. Your time is precious, and an organized bathroom can help make your glam routine as efficient as possible. Our bathroom may be tiny, but *shocker*—I don't wake up looking glamorous; I need a bit of help. I have my own little shelf in our small medicine cabinet over the sink that is my personal glam station. In three small clear bins, I have my razor, skin care products, and grooming products all neatly organized. Here's how to set up your own personal glam station:

1. **Clear:** Gather all your personal care and grooming products in one area.

2. **Sort:** Categorize your personal care products: everyday, special occasion, back stock.

3   **Assess:** Only everyday products belong in your glam station.

4. **Plan:** Consider how to contain the items so products are easily accessible.

Embracing the Beautiful Mess

Tidying up my mind and our physical space was a catalyst for self-discovery. It's been a beautifully messy ride. I've learned how to edit, simplify, and bring order to things. I've learned to wrestle with our family's definition of "just enough." I've learned how to experiment with routines and invite them to serve me, not control me. I've learned how to quiet the internal desire for more. I've been laying a foundation for personal growth, for aliveness.

As I write this, Emily and I have officially embarked on a new chapter of parenthood, transitioning from the early stages to the middle phase. It's a time of subtle shifts and delightful surprises and a few "Did that really just happen?" moments. The girls have started waking up a tad bit later, they're becoming a bit more independent, and the Great Bedtime Shuffle seems to be easing its grip on our evenings. Yet amid these changes, the girls still love to play, and they love for us to play alongside them. Play, in its purest form, is a profound gift that transcends age. I'm reminded that adults need time for play, too.

One of my favorite places to play with our girls is on the floor in front of their triple bunk bed. We recently added a thick rug pad underneath the vibrantly colored braided rug, which makes it extra comfortable and also muffles the sounds going down to the bedroom below, where our neighbors sleep. There are two large windows overlooking the city sidewalks below, and I love how the light pours into the space.

One of our favorite activities for that special spot is playing with blocks. The blocks we like best come in bright, happy colors and different shapes and sizes, and the set even comes with a storage box (which can be turned into a wooden car with movable wheels) and a lid for sorting shapes. Such smart toy engineering, and oh so tidy!

From towers to homes to city landscapes to castles, the possibilities of what to build are endless. At the end of the evening, with a busy day of teaching behind me, the open-endedness and peacefulness of block play is welcome. I love to sit and talk with the girls and see what they can dream up. What I think I love the most about block play is that there isn't one right answer. It's easy to change things, and to build off other people's ideas. There's joy in seeing how high you can build a tower, then when it comes crashing down, getting right back to building again. There are beautiful metaphors for life to be found in this.

In life, as in building a tower out of blocks, sometimes it feels like there's that *one block* holding everything in place. If you study the cover of this book, you'll see an example of this. Do you see that small blue circle block? What might happen if that one block were removed?

Removing that one block could unsettle the delicate balance

of blocks, causing other pieces to shift. What once felt stable and secure might become uncertain or precarious. Yet removing that block could also open up new possibilities, reveal a way to rebuild in a manner that might better align with your aspirations, values, and priorities.

Maybe you'll find that you can pull out one "block" in your life that you thought was holding everything together—a job, a relationship, a belief, a routine, a decision—and examine it anew. Maybe then you'll find that the entire tower you've built on that one thing doesn't have to fall apart. Or perhaps instead of trying to build a taller tower and stacking "more and more" pieces on top of one another until it collapses, you'll find that life is more like a game of Jenga, with a stable foundation where small blocks can be removed, rearranged, and reinserted in different spots, places where they fit even better, and that growth comes gradually.

What I'm getting at is that I know all too well that sometimes it feels like we're barely holding things together. I get overwhelmed, too, and struggle to maintain some semblance of stability. When I'm feeling that way, I try to remind myself that I always have choices. I can find ways to tidy up my life, even if the process feels shaky. Remember, life is a beautiful mess—I want you to courageously embrace the opportunity to restructure, tweak, and reimagine what could be possible.

Go on—tidy up your life!

ACKNOWLEDGMENTS

We all have a story, and there is power in sharing our journeys with one another. If you're in a chapter of life where you are struggling, it can be so helpful to share that with a friend, family member, or therapist. Talk to someone. Life—both the mundane moments and the moments filled with adventure—is something to be cherished. You are not alone, and your story matters. Thank you for reading part of mine.

Transforming my story from experiences and thoughts into jumbled words on a page and then ultimately into a published book has been a humbling experience. There's a team of people behind this self-described Tidy Dad whom I'd like to offer my sincere gratitude and thanks to.

I'd like to start by thanking all my teachers. You taught me to fall in love with books and helped me harness the power of writing. To my fourth grade teacher, Mrs. Nally, thanks for telling me that I was a good writer and teaching me how to use adjectives appropriately. To my high school history teacher, Mrs. Watkins, thanks for taking me on my first international field trip, where I got my first stamp in my passport. That trip opened my eyes to the world.

To my publishing team at Rodale and Penguin Random House, thank you for bringing this story to life. From the start, you championed and encouraged me and my ideas. To my editor, Marnie Cochran, thanks for your gentle and encouraging feedback, and for helping me tweak and re-tweak the organizational backbone of this book. Working with you was like a master class in writing, and you helped ground this book in both warmth and practicality. To Thomas Cherwin and Michelle Daniel, thank you for copyediting my ideas and making them clearer. To the design team and illustrator, thanks for taking this book beyond just words on a page and for capturing the essence of my words in visual form.

To my literary agents, Kathy Schneider and Jess Errera at the Jane Rotrosen Agency, thank you for believing that I had a unique voice and perspective to share with others, and for advising me on how to turn my ideas into a book. You both taught me that there's "what the book is about" and then there's "what the book is *really* about." Thank you for being my early readers and for your thoughtful feedback. To Diana Gill, thanks for helping me take my mess of ideas and craft them into a book proposal. You brought enthusiasm and energy to the project and understood that this story was about far more than just decluttering.

To my business coach, Christina Froeb, thanks for being a sounding board for my ideas and for helping me to name my priorities, craft "helicopter view" schedules, and reflect on my goals and progress. And thank you for frequently reminding me that "writing feels hard because it *is* hard."

To my manager, April Abrams, thanks for being protective of my time and energy, and for handling the barrage of emails, inquiries, and negotiations so that I could focus on writing. You also allow me to dump my creative ideas, and in many ways act as an improvisation partner, by responding with "Yes, and . . ." You helped me choose the right projects to say yes to, while maintaining enough margin to be able to get this book written without missing a deadline.

Thank you to all my friends who have been part of my journey over the years. I'm grateful that there are too many to name. To those I like to call my "Board of Directors," Shannon Nash, Kierra Grippa, and Patrick Murphy, thanks for listening to my ideas without laughing at me, and for the countless phone calls and texts. To Colt and Vanessa Emswiler and Travis and Jillian Timberlake, thanks for your prayers and encouragement. To Seth Whitton, thanks for saying "I noticed you've been using #tidydad in your Instagram posts; have you ever thought about changing your account name to 'Tidy Dad'?" That one question changed everything. To Zoe Rind, thanks for teaching me about the power of spending money to solve a problem. To Patty Morrissey, thanks for teaching me about Thirty-Day Experiments. To Jessie Crenshaw, thanks for your unwavering friendship throughout childhood, the awkward middle school years (remember you also wore a Backstreet Boys shirt on the first day of seventh grade), and beyond. Maybe I should have had you sign an NDA?

To my therapist, Suzanne Bien Bonet, thanks for telling me I could benefit from individual therapy sessions. You were right.

To my church community, thanks to Seth and Jenavene Bazacas, Dimetra Barrios, Kimetra Bryant, Brett Pontecorvo, and Teresa Murphy for prayerfully speaking into my life throughout the entire book writing process.

To the school communities where I've taught over the years, thank you for your friendship and support. You have made me a better teacher and writer. Thank you to Matt Kolman and Kevin Farrell for allowing me to experiment with a four-day teaching schedule while I was writing this book. To Leah Rizzo, Alana Howell, Katelyn Rosi, and Kate Athens, thanks for being among my earliest Tidy Dad supporters. To Barbara Pollack, thanks for showing as much interest in my writer's notebook as in my students' writer's notebooks. To Kim Moglia, thank you for your kindness and for sharing your perspective about pursuing the type of work that brings you joy. Our conversations helped to change the trajectory of my life. To my students, you've taught me more than you'll ever know. And to all my fellow teachers out there, your work is valuable, and you are making a difference.

To my Tidy Dad community, thank you for following my journey. Many of the ideas in this book first saw the light of day on my blog, website, and social media. Your support is what paved the way for this book to happen and motivates me to keep sharing my stories.

To my family, you truly know my messy side and love me anyway. To my dad, thanks for being a model for how to love your children well. Thanks for answering my phone calls, responding to my early morning texts, and for your willingness to listen to the thoughts and emotions that are flooding my brain. To my mom, thanks for watching the girls while Emily and I had writing weekends to finish editing this book. You brought calm to our chaos. Your enthusiasm and effervescent spirit are a joy to be around, and I'll always cherish our adventures together. To my sisters, Amanda and Kristin, thanks for allowing me to test out my Tidy Dad methods on your closets, for our hilarious group chats, and for understanding that the middle child really is the favorite. To my parents' spouses, Teri and Chris, thank you for being such a wonderful part of my parents' next chapters. To Audrey and Braden, I'll always cherish the memories from our years living in our "Queens Family Compound." To Trennis and Pam, thank you for raising Emily, and for moving her to Kentucky during middle school.

To Mabel, Matilda, and Margaret, sometimes you like to call me "Messy Dad," and I get it. Sometimes I call you my three little walking tornadoes. We see one another's mess, but that's one of the beautiful parts about being a family. I love being your dad.

To Emily, although you are not named as the co-author of this book, I couldn't have written it without you. From the beginning, we've always created content for Tidy Dad as a team. Thank you for reading and rereading chapter drafts and each time offering helpful critiques, edits, and perspective. I'm so grateful that we were assigned to sit next to each other on the first day of eighth grade. You have loved every (messy) version of me, from teenager to Tidy Dad and beyond. Thank you for being my number one cheerleader through it all. I love you forever and always.

ABOUT THE AUTHOR

Tyler Moore is the creator of the hugely popular "Tidy Dad" accounts on Instagram and TikTok, as well as the "Tidy Dad" website. A public school teacher in New York City, a husband, and the father of three young daughters, he has been featured on *Good Morning America* and in *The Washington Post, The New York Times, New York Post, Better Homes & Gardens Secrets of Getting Organized* magazine, Apartment Therapy, and many podcasts, including *HGTV Obsessed* and *Minimalist Moms.* During the school year, he lives with his wife, Emily, a pediatric occupational therapist, and daughters in Queens, New York. In the summer, they spend as much time as possible in their small but tidy cottage in the Poconos.

thetidydad.com
@tidydad